VUILLARD

SELF-PORTRAIT. 1891. Oil on panel, 11 x 8⅝".
Collection Mr. and Mrs. Paul Mellon, Upperville, Virginia

EDOUARD

VUILLARD

TEXT BY

STUART PRESTON

Harry N. Abrams, Inc., Publishers, New York

TO W. S. LIEBERMAN

ISBN 0–8109–1706–8
Library of Congress Catalog Card Number: 85–70922

Published in 1985 by Harry N. Abrams, Incorporated, New York
Also published in a leatherbound edition for The Easton Press,
Norwalk, Connecticut. All rights reserved. This is a concise
edition of Stuart Preston's Vuillard, *originally published in*
1971. No part of the contents of this book may be reproduced
without the written permission of the publisher.

Printed and bound in Japan

CONTENTS

———

E Vuillard

No maxim is infallible, but it has often been said, and with good reason, that an artist's work best explains the artist himself. Nevertheless, as the sole ground on which to explain any artist's significance in the history of art, a study of his work alone is clearly inadequate. It is equally necessary to know something about the man himself, even in the case of such an apparently impersonal artist as the French painter Edouard Vuillard (1868–1940), whose life was so outwardly lacking in incident. The work comes first, but his high place among modern painters must also be judged in the light of the life he led—the historical, intellectual, and personal circumstances that molded his daily existence. Not only his artistic origins must be looked into, but his contacts with contemporaries and the influence he exerted both in his own lifetime and afterward.

"I have never been anything but a spectator," he once said, and in an important sense this is true.

Vuillard's life—serene, comfortable, warmed by the affection and admiration of those for whom he cared most—remained that of a late nineteenth-century French petty bourgeois. Emotional storms and crises of conscience may have raged beneath that placid surface, but of such we know almost nothing—nothing, that is, until the opening of his private journal, promised for the 1980s. Perhaps not then. As of the moment, we have the image of a timid, reticent, even secretive individual; a dedicated bachelor attached above all to his mother, his "muse" as he called her, with whom he lived until her death in 1928 when he was sixty years old. He may have been reserved and averse to publicity, not to speak of notoriety, but he was far from being unsocial or solitary. He had a close, devoted, and increasingly wide circle of friends, most of them painters such as his brother-in-law Ker-Xavier Roussel, Pierre Bonnard, and many others; and he ventured further into

1. Left: An early photographic self-portrait

the larger Paris world than is generally supposed.

So much for the public picture that Vuillard presents. There is nothing faintly dramatic about his uneventful round of works and days. But it also happens that he was a great painter whose art, elixir-like, transformed the ordinary surroundings of his life into visions of eternal beauty. Such subject matter as he chose, mostly interiors with figures and, later, highly wrought commissioned portraits, had little intrinsically inspiring about it. Yet he succeeded in glorifying the commonplace by an extraordinary aesthetic and poetic concentration, finding it beautiful to paint because he thought it beautiful to the eye. Even if he was not the kind of man to reveal himself personally in his art, through his art he revealed the world he

2. Right: PORTRAIT OF THE ART-IST WITH HIS FRIEND VAROQUI. c. 1888–90. Oil on canvas, 36 × 28″. *The Metropolitan Museum of Art, New York City. Gift of Alex M. Lewyt, 1955*

lived in with distinction and charm that command admiration.

Nevertheless Vuillard's artistic reputation has, like that of other painters, suffered ups and downs through the years. From 1890 to about 1900, the decade of his brilliant, daring, proto-Fauve figure paintings and captivating and poetic decorations, he was regarded almost as a revolutionary, and certainly considered the most talented member of the Nabi group of painters. Then, after 1900, so his critics insist, the vital spark of his work dimmed. By neglecting fully to exploit his discoveries he faltered, relying too much on natural gifts and refined taste to take advantage of the great pictorial revolutions of the early twentieth century. It would be difficult indeed to imagine a Cubist or a Surrealist Vuillard. Yet critics argue that in becoming a sort of court painter to a wealthy and no more than fairly cultured section of Parisian society he lost his original élan and power by too willingly identifying himself with the social group he served. It is true that Vuillard took a conservative turn in about 1900, and that for the next thirty years he led a retiring life, rarely exhibiting publicly after 1914. Between 1910 and the late 1930s, when one revolutionary artistic experiment followed another in dizzy succession, he became increasingly outmoded and unregarded.

However, interest was reawakened—for the young, awakened—by the large retrospective of his work (1890–1910) at the Musée des Arts Décoratifs in Paris in 1938, two years before his death. For the first time the beauty and humanity of his youthful achievement could be judged by a wide public. Today his work is more highly esteemed than ever. Time has a way of revising hasty judgments and allows us to see past things afresh, both in themselves and as part of a living heritage.

Edouard Vuillard's origins were simple enough. He was born of a Parisian family on 11 November 1868 at Cuiseaux, Saône-et-Loire, where his father, a retired army officer, held the post of tax collector. Madame Vuillard, born Marie Michaud of a family of textile designers, and twenty-seven years younger than her husband, had previously borne two children, Marie, who was to marry Vuillard's closest friend, Ker-Xavier Roussel, and Alexandre, who took up his father's

3. ROUSSEL FAMILY. c. 1895. Oil on canvas, 19 × 25⅝″. *Collection Mrs. Charles Vidor, New York City*

4. Right: THE ARTIST'S MOTHER. 1896. Black chalk, 25 × 18″. *Collection Mr. and Mrs. Norton Simon, Los Angeles*

5. THE WIDOW'S VISIT. c. 1893. Oil on paper mounted on panel, 19¾×24¾″. *The Art Gallery of Ontario, Toronto. Purchase 1937*

6. WOMAN IN BED. c. 1891. Watercolor, 6×8¾″. *Estate of Ailsa Mellon Bruce*

career of soldiering and died in 1928. Young Edouard seems to have been a normal child, piously brought up and possibly more quiet than the average. In 1878 he and his family moved to Paris. In 1884 his father died, leaving Madame Vuillard in straitened circumstances. She set up modestly as a corsetiere, a business operated in a succession of family apartments, all of them in the neighborhood of the Rue St. Honoré. Vuillard's sister taught him to read, and his first school was under the direction of the Marist Fathers, a Catholic teaching order. He then entered Ecole Rocroy and later attended the Lycée Condorcet, where he met Roussel in 1884. The Lycée was one of the best schools in Paris, producing a remarkable number of leaders in the intellectual and political life of the Third Republic. The poet Stéphane Mallarmé taught English there until 1884, and it was later attended by Marcel Proust.

Attendance at the Condorcet was to be a decisive

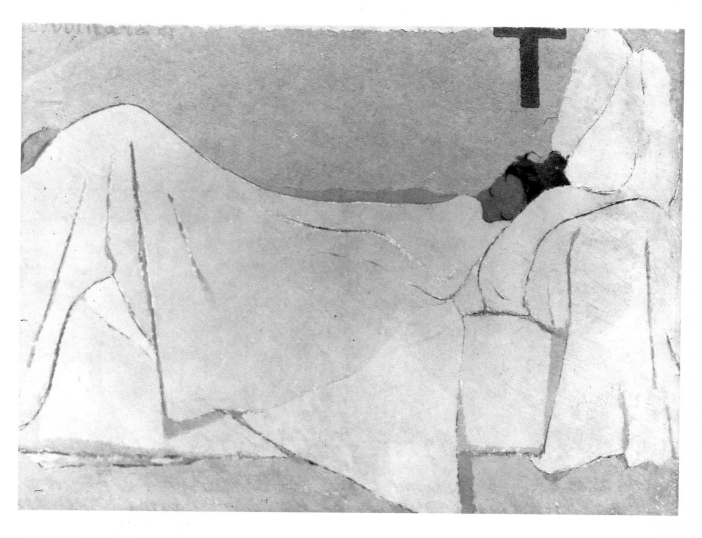

7. IN BED. 1891. Oil on canvas, 29⅛ × 36¼″. *Musée National d'Art Moderne, Paris*

move for Vuillard. There, influenced by the future painters Roussel and Maurice Denis, as well as by the brilliant young Lugné-Poë, who was destined to be a catalyst of all the arts in his role of actor-manager of the Théâtre de l'Oeuvre in the 1890s, he abandoned his original desire for a military career and took up painting. Nothing known about the young Vuillard anticipates this startling change of direction. His reply to a question about this transformation is hardly illuminating: "I should like to say as Degas did: On Sundays they took us to the Louvre. My brother slid about on the waxed floors and I looked at the paintings." Even if this wishful remark had been true, it would not have indicated exceptional precocity or a particular leaning toward the career of an artist. But something deep in his nature must have drawn him to art. Possibly the influence of heredity or environment had something to do with it. Traditions of design

8. PAYSAGE EN ÎLE DE FRANCE. c. 1894. Oil on panel, 7⅜ × 10″. *Collection Mr. and Mrs. Paul Mellon, Upperville, Virginia*

9. THE ARTIST'S MOTHER. c. 1891. Oil on cardboard, 8½ × 6½". *Collection Mr. and Mrs. William Goetz, Los Angeles*

were in his family. Both his grandfather and an uncle designed textiles, and his whole youth was surrounded by the figured materials that crowded his mother's workroom. In any event, always affected by stronger wills than his own, he fell in enthusiastically with the plans of his friends, who largely helped him discover his vocation and spurred him on once it had been found. What is more, he had the loyal and sympathetic support of his mother, no stranger to artistic creativity.

Of that remarkable lady Pierre Véber, an early friend of Vuillard, writes: "Hers was a figure of extraordinary purity and nobility. Marvellous was her tenderness for our friend. She believed in his mission and consecrated herself to it with a conscientiousness and self-denial almost without precedent. It was thanks to her that Edouard Vuillard became the perfect artist whom we know. . . . To her this powerful artist owes the inviolable modesty which he evinced even in the face of unhoped-for triumphs." Thus backed and protected, Vuillard in 1887 both discovered his Rubicon and crossed it.

Vuillard and Roussel first studied under a forgotten

10. THE FERRY MAN. 1897. Oil on cardboard, 20½ × 29½". *Musée National d'Art Moderne, Paris*

11. GARDEN AT CANNES. 1902. Oil on canvas, 29⅝×41⅛″. *The Metropolitan Museum of Art, New York City. Gift of Mr. and Mrs. Nathan L. Halpern, 1965*

painter, Ulysse-Diogène-Napoléon Maillart, who occupied Delacroix's old studio in the Place Furstenberg and who, despite his ambitious nomenclature, failed to achieve fame. The next year Vuillard enrolled at the Ecole des Beaux-Arts, supervised by the most hidebound of conservative painters, Jean-Léon Gérôme, famous for the deadly precision with which he reconstructed Oriental scenes. His unimaginative teaching alienated Vuillard from academic art for life. Nonetheless, the still lifes he painted there, delicate but hardly distinguishable from work by other students, are signed "Vuillard—Pupil of Gérôme." Dissatisfied by the Beaux-Arts, and probably urged on by Pierre Bonnard, he switched to a well-known art school, the Académie Julian. There, despite the head teacher being the egregious Bouguereau, Vuillard

found himself in a hotbed of gifted young rebels, notably Bonnard and Maurice Denis, as well as Paul Sérusier, Armand Séguin, Paul Ranson, Jan Verkade, Henri Ibels, and Félix Vallotton—in short, the Nabis of the immediate future, the new generation knocking at the door of the old and about to break it down.

Ardent and gay, intelligent and sensible, living simply and intensely and with a vague eye to the future, these mild, determined young rebels banded themselves together under the name "Nabis," a term derived from the Hebrew word for prophet bestowed on them by the poet Cazalis. They would meet in the evenings, endlessly discuss painting, and indulge in minor, slightly childish mystifications such as wearing Oriental costume, using passwords, and giving each other nicknames. Vuillard was called the *Zouave* be-

12. Félix Vallotton. THE FIVE PAINTERS (from left to right: Vallotton, Bonnard, Vuillard, Cottet, Roussel). 1902. Oil on canvas, $56\frac{1}{4} \times 73\frac{5}{8}''$. *Kunstmuseum, Winterthur*

13. Maurice Denis. HOMAGE TO CÉZANNE (from left to right: Redon, Vuillard, Mellerio, Vollard, Denis, Sérusier, Ranson, Roussel, Bonnard, Madame Denis). 1900. Oil on canvas, $70\frac{7}{8} \times 94\frac{1}{2}''$. *Musée National d'Art Moderne, Paris*

14. Left: PORTRAIT OF FÉLIX VALLOTTON. 1900. Distemper on cardboard mounted on panel, 29⅝ × 19⅝". *Musée National d'Art Moderne, Paris*

15. Below: LITTLE GIRLS WALKING. 1891. Oil on canvas, 32 × 25⅝". *Collection Mrs. Charles Stachelberg, New York City*

cause of his short military-style beard. Bonnard was called *japonard,* Sérusier *à la barbe rutilante,* Denis *le Nabi aux belles icônes,* and Vallotton, who joined the group in 1894, *le Nabi étranger.* Occasionally they would dine with Madame Vuillard, but their usual meeting places were a restaurant in the Impasse Brady and the studio of Ranson, referred to as the "Temple," with Madame Ranson as "the light of the Temple." None of their antics were meant to be taken too seriously, but their discussions about painting and its future were serious indeed.

With no other common aesthetic credo except a general dissatisfaction with both academicism and Impressionism, and an unformulated wish to reform painting, the Nabis did not survive long as a close-knit body of artists. The group had more or less disbanded by the turn of the century; each member went his separate way, but each bore the imprint of his early associations. From the beginning Vuillard, Bonnard, and Roussel were somewhat separated from the others, who were all characterized by a religious interest of one sort or another. Denis was a devout Catholic whose subjects were usually religious; Sérusier was devoted to various mystical philosophies —a combination of Swedenborgianism and theosophy

with Catholicism; Ranson was a theosophist; and almost all later recruits to the group, with the exception of Vallotton, were involved in religious experience. For this reason, many discussions of the Nabis emphasize the larger religious group of painters at the expense of Vuillard, Roussel, Bonnard, and Vallotton. Indeed, some treatments and exhibitions even omit some or all of these four, but this is unjustified. While they were together they presented a united front in their effort to restore imagination and

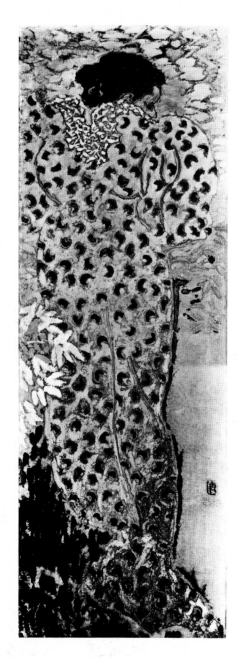

feeling to art, which they thought had been too long impoverished intellectually. They called themselves prophets, and in Paul Gauguin they found a Messiah.

In their vaguely expressed but deeply felt convictions about Impressionism's inadequacies the Nabis made the best and only possible choice in backing Gauguin as their leader. Gauguin had actually, in concert with Emile Bernard, elaborated a new aesthetic doctrine in tune with theirs. He refused to subscribe to the Impressionists' docile copying of nature, insisting that an artist be free to choose what was, to him, significant in nature and transform it into something entirely personal by means of what he called "a synthesis of form and color derived from the observation of the dominant element only." To this end he coaxed subject matter into rhythmical designs by boldly juxtaposing patches of flat color organized in willful and frankly decorative ways. Originated in 1888 in Brittany, where Gauguin was then living, this doctrine became known as the Synthetic-Symbolist style. It was to have enormous effect on painters rebelling against Impressionism.

16. Pierre Bonnard. THE PEIGNOIR. c. 1890. Oil on velvet, $60\frac{5}{8} \times 21\frac{1}{4}$. *Musée National d'Art Moderne, Paris*

17. YOUNG GIRL SEATED. 1891. Brush drawing, $7\frac{7}{8} \times 7\frac{1}{8}''$. *Collection Mr. and Mrs. Alfred R. Stern, New York City*

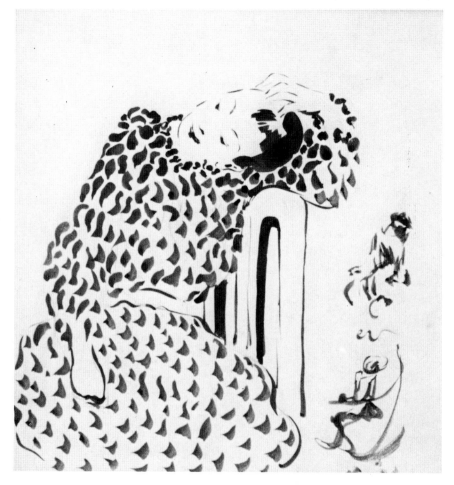

Taking liberties with the visual world and instilling poetic meaning into subject matter came as a revelation to the Nabis when they saw Gauguin's paintings in an unofficial exhibition held in a restaurant, the Café Volpini, at the Paris Exposition of 1889. One of them, Paul Sérusier, provided an even closer link with the Master, for he had had a painting lesson with Gauguin in Brittany and had learned from him that art should become "a mirror wherein is reflected the state of soul of the artist." Gauguin further declared that the Impressionists "pursued their searches in accordance with the eye and not toward the mysterious center of thought, and consequently fell into scientific rationalizations." The latter were anathema to Gauguin, an artist of instinct if ever there was one. Without constructing theories, he believed firmly that form and color, light, shadow, and line had intrinsic meaning that could serve poetic and spiritual ends. Technically, of course, this arbitrary use of such elements looked ahead to an abstract style where color, "being an enigmatic thing in the sensations it gives us," could be made to symbolize the artist's inner emotions. The doctrine of Gauguin was summed up in the already mentioned famous outdoor lesson where Sérusier, under Gauguin's direction, painted *Paysage dans le Bois d'Amour,* the landscape that soon became known as *"The Talisman."* The young painter, who had been completely won over to Gauguin's views, brought the painting back to Paris for the edification of his friends. This crucial episode is best recounted in an article by Maurice Denis entitled "The Influence of Paul Gauguin."

It was late in 1888 that the name of Gauguin was revealed to us by Sérusier on his return from Pont-Aven. It was then that he showed us, somewhat mysteriously, the cover of a cigar box on which one could vaguely distinguish a landscape, synthetically represented in violet, red, green and other pure colors just as they came out of the tube with barely an admixture of white. "How do you see that tree?" said Gauguin. "Very green? Then use green, the richest green on your palette. And that shadow? Bluish? Don't hesitate to paint it as blue as possible. And for those red leaves, vermilion." We thus came to realize that each work of art was a transposition of visual facts, a caricature so to speak, the impassioned equivalent of a visual impression made on one. . . . This method

18. Ker-Xavier Roussel. THE SEAMSTRESSES. c. 1894. Oil on canvas, $44\frac{1}{8} \times 30\frac{1}{8}''$. *Collection Mr. and Mrs. Arthur G. Altschul, New York City*

19. Maurice Denis. ANNUNCIATION. 1891. Oil on canvas, $10\frac{5}{8} \times 16\frac{1}{8}''$. *Rijksmuseum Kröller-Müller, Otterlo (Holland)*

20. Paul Sérusier. PAYSAGE DANS LE BOIS D'AMOUR: LE "TALISMAN". 1888. Oil on panel, 10⅝ × 8⅝". *Private collection, Paris*

cleared away all the obstacles which simple copying imposed on our painterly instincts. . . . If one were permitted to paint in bright scarlet a tree that looked reddish brown, then why not translate plastically, and exaggerate, impressions such as those substantiated in the metaphors of poets, going so far as to deform the curvature of a back, exaggerate the pearly white of a carnation or stiffen the symmetry of the branches of a tree. This procedure suddenly explained the whole Louvre to us—the Primitives, and Rubens and Veronese.

The notorious little picture, with its brilliant juxtaposition of pure colors and no more than casual resemblance to nature, was a revelation indeed—the Nabis' Road to Damascus. It operated on their senses, as one of them said, "like the removal of a cataract."

Among the Nabis the lesson of *"The Talisman,"* a miracle-working object if ever there was one, fell on fertile ground. Sérusier's role as John the Baptist

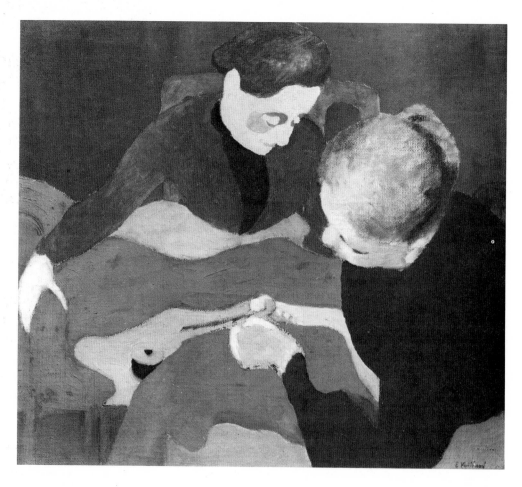

21. THE DRESSMAKERS. 1891. Oil on canvas, 18¾ × 21⅝". *Collection Mrs. Charles Vidor, New York City*

succeeded beyond all expectation, although each Nabi interpreted it according to his own temperament. Maurice Denis, the chief Nabi theoretician, went so far as to redefine the art of painting. "It must be recalled," he sweepingly declared, echoing Gauguin's theories, "that a picture, before being a warhorse, a nude or any other anecdote, is essentially a flat surface covered with colors arranged in a certain order." This statement may sound mild enough today. But it was a rebellious war cry in 1890, a shout of defiance to the solidly entrenched fortresses of academicism. These simple words broke radically with the past and foretold the future. In subscribing to Denis's definition, using color in purely instinctive ways and representing nature expressively rather than literally, the Nabis, and especially Vuillard, in the early 1890s anticipated the Fauves by at least fifteen years. Whatever else the Nabis may have been—and by no means were all of them inspired performers—their various reactions against Impressionism led directly to what we know today as modern art. For later artists carried the Nabi liberation of form and color to its logical abstract conclusions, to further revolutionary experiments.

Someone once gave the Nabi pedigree as follows: "Fathered by Gauguin out of literary symbolism with Sérusier as the midwife." This puts things neatly enough, and we have seen how Gauguin, by pulling

23. Odilon Redon. PORTRAIT OF MADEMOISELLE VIOLETTE HEYMANN. 1910. Pastel, 28¾ × 36⅜". *The Cleveland Museum of Art. Hinman B. Hurlbut Collection*

the rug from under simple naturalism, restored imaginative values to art. Furthermore, in specifically technical matters his radical innovations included the virtual elimination of atmosphere, local color, and deep perspective, the imposition of design on visual facts instead of the other way round, and the use of strong, simple, contrasted colors broken up into broad areas rather than the Impressionist profusion of subtle rainbow hues. The young Vuillard was to put all of these technical innovations to his own pur-

24. Odilon Redon. PORTRAIT OF VUILLARD. 1900. Lithograph, 7⅝ × 5⅞". *Bibliothèque Nationale, Cabinet des Estampes, Paris*

poses, although in a wider sense he cannot be considered a Gauguin follower. "For Edouard Vuillard," wrote Maurice Denis, "the crisis provoked by Gauguin's ideas was of short duration. He owes him, however, the solidity of Gauguin's system of touches on which he built up the intense and delicate charm of his compositions." Nor was Vuillard of the stuff that revolutionaries and adventurers are made. His wilder shores extended no further than Paris and the suburbs. Nor could Oceania have held much appeal to this quiet, timid bourgeois whose life was locked into a secure framework of family, close friends, and the studio.

So much for what Gauguin taught the Nabis—a method of simplification and abstraction that was the complete antithesis of Impressionism, and a style capable of being charged with poetic and emotional associations. But what, one may ask, has literary Symbolism got to do with the new style, and what in fact was Symbolism? At any historical moment avant-garde art and literature have more in common than might at first be evident, existing as they do in the same intellectual climate and linked in similar ways of expression to similar ends. Thus, in France during the decade after 1885, the surge of imagination against naturalism launched by Gauguin, Puvis de Chavannes, Gustave Moreau, and other painters found its counterpart in the imaginative work of Symbolist writers who anathematized both the ruthless realism of novelists such as Zola and the objective, impersonal preciosity of the Parnassian school of poetry. Leading this counteroffensive against the scientific and positivist spirit of the age was the writer Stéphane Mallarmé, "Prince of Poets" and high priest of literary Symbolism. But we are not concerned here with his exquisite and hermetic poetry. What does concern us is the vital influence, both in person and as a purveyor of ideas, that this hero of letters exerted on the Nabis, and particularly on Vuillard, who knew and revered Mallarmé.

"The essence of Symbolism," writes Sir Maurice Bowra, "is its insistence on a world of ideal beauty,

25. SELF-PORTRAIT IN A STRAW HAT. c. 1892. Oil on canvas, 14½ × 11". *Collection Mr. and Mrs. Ralph F. Colin, New York City*

26. RED AND WHITE CARNATIONS. 1894. Oil on canvas, 19 × 24". *Collection Catherine M. and John W. Warner, Washington, D.C.*

27. Right: TOULOUSE-LAUTREC IN THE AISLE. c. 1895. Oil on canvas, 10½ × 8¼". *Collection Mme Raphaël Salem, Paris*

and its conviction that this is realized through art." And in evoking ideal beauty art should suggest rather than describe. Its concern lies with impressions, intuitions, sensations, not bare fact. For to name something flatly is to destroy it. Such ideas were expounded by Mallarmé at the famous gatherings at his apartment in the Rue de Rome, where entranced disciples congregated regularly on Tuesday evenings between the years 1885 and 1894. Vuillard was often present and became somewhat of a favorite with the poet, visiting him at his country house at Valvins, on the Seine near Fontainebleau. In fact, Mallarmé wished him to illustrate his poem *Hérodiade*, a project unfortunately never carried out. There can be no question but that Symbolism as preached by Mallarmé deeply affected the young painter. Hence the veiled meanings and general air of ambiguous mystery that characterize many of Vuillard's paintings of the early 1890s, which tend to clothe an idea in perceptible form, to create an effect rather than tell a story. Like Mallarmé's more obscure poetry, these little interiors with figures are apprehended rather than comprehended.

Another Symbolist principle was that of "reticence," a code of austere behavior which led to the

28. TOULOUSE-LAUTREC AT THE NATANSONS AT VILLENEUVE-SUR-YONNE. c. 1897. Oil on cardboard, 15⅝ × 11¾". *Musée Toulouse-Lautrec, Albi*

29. PORTRAIT OF MADAME BONNARD. c. 1895–1900.
Oil and turpentine on panel, 16⅜ × 12½". *Collection Mr. and Mrs.
Paul Mellon, Upperville, Virginia*

30. THE ART TALK. 1898. Distemper on cardboard, 10¾ ×
15¾". *Collection Mrs. Harriet Weiner, New York City*

creation of art for the happy few rather than for the marketplace. With Mallarmé's statement, "I have kept my secret. I have not betrayed myself to the multitude," Vuillard found himself temperamentally in full accord. For reality was a private affair, what one represented for oneself, a credo responsible for the somewhat narcissistic air of Vuillard's early genre scenes, which are more extensions of himself than literal transcriptions of given subjects. In fact, so reticent was he that his more hard-headed friends, notably Lugné-Poë, were at some pains to persuade him to sell at all in the 1890s. Finally, in their reaction against naturalism, the Symbolists believed that the imagination, not the eye, retained the form of things—a belief Vuillard found in tune with his own. He preferred to sift subject matter through the mind before painting it, thus keeping only that which was of significance to him.

The Nabis also held older Symbolist painters in high esteem, especially Odilon Redon. "I have the greatest admiration for Redon," wrote Bonnard. "What strikes me most in his work is the blending of two almost opposite features; a very pure plastic substance and a very mysterious expression. . . . Our entire generation has experienced his charm and received his advice." This admiring point of view was shared by Denis: "The lesson of Redon was his incapacity to paint anything which did not represent a state of soul." And although Vuillard never crossed over into the utter fantasy of Redon's art, he cherished the older man as a friend, made a grave and touching portrait of him in 1901, and in later years he and his mother visited Redon in his country house on the estuary of the Gironde River.

Puvis de Chavannes was another contributing force to Vuillard's development. He admired the decorative grandeur of Puvis's mural paintings, his idealizing tendencies, and the tender eloquence of his figures, so warmly human in their simple poses and gestures. With the passage of time, and the absorption of these diverse initial influences into an independent style, overt evidences of Symbolism gradually disappear from Vuillard's art. But its importance for his beginnings cannot be minimized.

During the 1890s, Vuillard rapidly rose to the summit of his powers, a remarkable feat considering the lateness of his start as a painter and the few years of rather haphazard training in various academies. In fact, 1890 itself was the crucial year of Vuillard's

life. Spurred on by Meissonier's rejection of one of
his still lifes for the Salon, he broke away from conservative realism and asserted the charm and novelty
of a new style which expressed and satisfied his inner
being. Perhaps this is the moment to describe how
he struck contemporaries and close friends who
observed him in familiar surroundings and in the little
studio at 28 Rue Pigalle, which he shared at that time
with Bonnard, Denis, and Lugné-Poë. "It was there,"
Lugné-Poë wrote, "that the Nabis were born—those
chaste prophets of painting who cut themselves, like
a new branch, from the proud trunk of Signac, Seurat,
and Pissarro." He also noticed what individualized
Vuillard among the Nabis. "Vuillard, whose friendship, like that of Bonnard, I owe to Denis, was quite
different. He was delicate by nature, and had none of
the fanaticism which could be glimpsed beneath
Denis's peaceable manner. In Vuillard's company one
was at peace with the world. Nothing could be more
harmonious than his life and his actions. He was un-
affectedly good. His exquisite modesty caused him
always to hide behind the merits of others."

Much the same impression was made on the Dutch
Nabi, Verkade, who thought Vuillard "profoundly
French, in the style of Saint-François de Sales, whom
he deeply resembled—he never expressed himself in
a positive fashion for fear of not being in the right."
The poet Romain Coolus detected regional influences
on him. "Vuillard," he wrote, "a native of the Jura,
belongs to that ancient French province which has
marked characteristics, especially mental concentration. . . . They [men of the Jura] have inherited a
disposition to survey life with gravity, to weigh their
judgments long before pronouncing them, to do or
to make nothing hastily. I have often been struck
with the importance Vuillard attached to the word
importance. Things that Parisian skepticism would have

33. Photograph of Madame Vuillard at breakfast with her grandchildren, c. 1905

34. WOMAN WITH A BOWL. c. 1897. Oil on cardboard, $23\frac{1}{4} \times 21\frac{1}{4}''$. *Collection André Meyer, New York City*

cheerfully dismissed as secondary were treasured in his mind and subjected to special consideration."

Equally enlightening is the account in Paul Signac's diary of a visit paid later in this decade.

Vuillard took me to his home—he's a sensitive and intelligent person and a highly strung, questioning painter. You feel that he has an unresting passion for art. His way of life has a dignity that commands respect. He lives with his mother, keeps well away from the cliques, and does his work in their small family apartment. He showed me sketches from every phase of his revolution. His deftly noted interiors have great charm. He has a marvelous understanding of the timbre of things. They're the work of a fine painter, those many-colored panels, predominantly dark in key, but always with an explosion of bright color that somewhere reestablishes the harmony of the whole picture. The contrast of tone, the skillfully achieved chiaroscuro—these balance a scheme of color which, though often gray and languid in effect, is always unusual and delicate—almost unhealthily so, in fact. Of course Vuillard, as a painter, has freed himself completely from that reality with which we others have to contend. Each artist must take his inspiration, to a certain extent, direct from nature; Vuillard balances too far on the side of fantasy.

Even though Signac's robustly realistic aesthetic lacked total sympathy with Vuillard's, this is a scrupulously honest and subtle analysis of the latter's style in the late 1890s.

By nature Vuillard was an unusually silent, bottled-up person, revealing his private thoughts to very few friends and only rarely, but memorably, exploding in fits of rage. Tormented by over-refined scruples, he long hesitated before showing his work. "I must look out," he said to Lugné-Poë, who acted as a sort of impresario for him. "These well-meaning patrons may disturb my routine. As yet I am not formed—at least, I hope not. And here they are accepting things done anyhow as finished work. True, I am compelled to earn my living, but one must be strong not to lose oneself in the process. . . ."

Confidence in his own powers grew slowly and tortuously. "I suffer too much in my life and my work," he wrote to Denis. "It is not while I am working that I think of the technique of picture

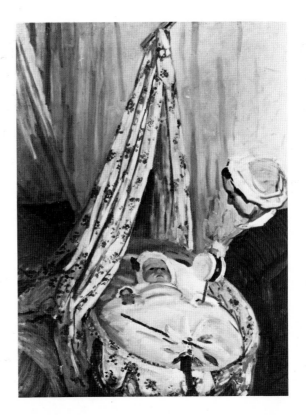

35. Claude Monet. JEAN MONET IN HIS CRADLE. 1867. Oil on canvas, 45¾ × 35″. *Collection Mr. and Mrs. Paul Mellon, Upperville, Virginia*

making or of immediate satisfaction. To speak generally, it is not while I am doing this or that that I consider the quality of my actions (you have only to think of my diffidence and my character). Whatever I have the happiness to be working at, it is because there is an idea in me in which I have faith. . . . The important thing is that my faith has produced works. And I admit that is work. In general, I have a horror or rather a blue funk of general ideas which I haven't discovered for myself, but I don't deny their value. I prefer to be humble rather than pretend to understanding."

Vuillard's friends refused to allow him to hide behind this diffidence; they determined that the talents they admired in him should be widely proclaimed. First and foremost among his backers was the group of progressive artists and writers associated with that famous magazine, *La Revue Blanche,* founded in 1891 by Alfred, Alexandre, and Thadée Natanson, sons of a banker. It would be impossible to exaggerate the importance of this literary, dramatic, and artistic review in European intellectual life during its twelve-year existence. It put Symbolism and the Nabis on the map, so to speak; Tolstoy, Ibsen, and Strindberg were introduced to French readers in its exciting

36. THE MEAL. c. 1899. Oil on canvas, $27\frac{1}{2} \times 28''$. *Collection Henry P. McIlhenny, Philadelphia*

37. Photograph of Misia and Thadée Natanson, Rue St. Florentin, 1898

pages; it published Gauguin's *Noa-Noa* in 1897; and in 1901 it carried the first critical article to appear on Picasso. Léon Blum wrote about books and plays for it; Maurice Denis dealt with painting; Debussy discussed music, and the witty playwright Tristan Bernard contributed to the sporting page.

The constellation of contributors to the *Revue Blanche* was a dazzling one, including as it did André Gide, Rémy de Gourmont, Alfred Jarry, Pierre Louÿs, Paul Claudel, Guillaume Apollinaire, Maurice Maeterlinck, Octave Mirbeau, Marcel Proust, Emile Verhaeren, Maxim Gorki, and Paul Verlaine, all of them published here, as that great editor Félix Fenéon stated, "in their bloom and their prime." More to the point, here is the active collaboration sought by the *Revue Blanche* with painters. Hence, not only numerous proselytizing articles about them but color lithographs as well by Vuillard, Bonnard, Toulouse-Lautrec, Vallotton, and Edvard Munch enlivened the already lively pages. The *Revue Blanche* also ran a little art gallery on its premises in the Rue des Martyrs and there, in 1891, gave Vuillard his first one-man show.

The muse, and in many ways the dominating figure in the *Revue Blanche* world, was Thadée Natanson's wife, the famous Misia. She later married the Spanish painter José Maria Sert, and was one of the most re-

38. MODEL IN A BIG HAT. c. 1900. Oil on canvas, 29 ×
23". *Collection Mr. and Mrs. Albert Dreitzer, New York City*

39. MISIA (LADY WITH A HAT). c. 1900. Oil on panel,
26 × 30½". *Collection Mrs. Charles Goldman, New York City*

40. WOMAN IN AN INTERIOR. 1907. Oil on cardboard, 16¾ × 20¼". *Collection Mr. and Mrs. Leo M. Rogers, New York City*

41. Eugène Carrière. MATERNITÉ. c. 1887. Oil on canvas, 11¾ × 15¾". *The Louvre, Paris*

markable women of her generation. A gifted pianist, cherished as a child by Liszt and a pupil of Fauré, she became in later life a practical and discriminating patron of the arts. Renoir, Lautrec, Vuillard, and Bonnard painted portraits of her; Verlaine and Mallarmé wrote poems to her; she helped launch Diaghilev's Ballet Russe in France and rapidly became a power in Paris between 1890 and 1940. But when Vuillard first knew her in the 1890s she lived entirely among writers, musicians, and artists, her great social position lying ahead of her. She must have been something of a siren and held Vuillard under her spell. In her memoirs she claims he was in love with her, and this may well have been true. In any event, the story she tells of his declaration to her sounds likely. One day when walking with her he suddenly burst into tears. No word was spoken. Remembering how moved she had been, she summed up the little episode in the words, "Nothing was lost by this understanding being a wordless one." They both would have agreed with Voltaire's line (from one of his few poems in English), "True love is best by silence known." Misia and Vuillard continued on friendly terms throughout his life, but their real intimacy ceased after 1900.

If the activity revolving about the *Revue Blanche* sustained Vuillard intellectually during these early years, a more specifically artistic stimulus was his ardent collaboration with Lugné-Poë's Théâtre de l'Oeuvre, founded in 1893. Actually Vuillard chose its name because of his being, according to Lugné, "the most interested in the theatre and the best judge of these matters." He both illustrated programs and designed sets of which the best known were those for Ibsen's *Rosmersholm*, on which Bonnard also worked. Alas, nothing remains of this décor but Lugné's words of praise: "It was the scenery of the second act which stamped the note of intimacy and distinction on our set. Vuillard surpassed himself in ingenuity and economic invention in creating atmosphere and scenic decoration."

Vuillard gained valuable experience from this work in the theater. He learned how to use distemper, which became his favorite medium. Being obliged to cover large areas with figures against backgrounds was to be a useful lesson when it came to painting the big decorative panels which many judges consider his greatest work. Moreover, he learned how to dramatize a composition. Vuillard can hardly be considered a

42. WOMAN SEATED UNDER A LAMP. 1899. Oil on canvas, 28 × 27″. *Collection Mr. and Mrs. John A. Beck, Houston*

43. THE FIRST STEPS. 1902. Oil on canvas, 20 × 14¼″. *Collection Mrs. Albert D. Lasker, New York City*

44. THE DRESSMAKER'S SHOP. c. 1893. Oil on canvas, 18¼ × 45½″. *Collection Mrs. Charles Stachelberg, New York City*

45. THE BENCH. 1895. Oil on cardboard, 14¼ × 21½". *Private collection, Paris*

46. Photograph of Madame Vuillard shelling peas, 1905

theatrical painter, but there is something about his disposition of figures and his clever use of artificial light that recall the artifice of the stage.

All was then grist to Vuillard's mill. "At that time," he recalled years later, "I was ready for everything. I took on the oddest jobs, anything which presented itself . . . working for the love of the thing, and also to earn my living." And also because the Nabis, perhaps influenced by William Morris's Arts and Crafts movement in England, believed in versatility. Vuillard, commissioned by Samuel Bing, the famous Art Nouveau dealer, made designs for Tiffany stained glass, and for plates with images from contemporary French life featuring young women. He was never truly an Art Nouveau artist, but the style itself, with its emphasis on movement and convoluted design, does contain elements of Nabi aesthetic.

Unlike the other Nabis, Vuillard was largely indifferent to theory and would remain silent while his friends heatedly discussed the nature of art. Significantly, the only period in his painting life when he followed strictly theoretical ideas was at the very beginning, in and around 1890, when he painted those startling little pictures in bright patches of pure Gauguinesque color—detail is eliminated and willfully decorative design overwhelms and flattens the subject matter. These daring proto-Fauve pictures directly reflect the teaching of *"The Talisman"* and obey

47. MADAME ROUSSEL AND JACQUES ROUSSEL. 1903. Oil on cardboard, $42\frac{1}{4} \times 32\frac{3}{4}''$. *Collection the Vuillard family, Paris*

48. MODEL IN THE STUDIO. c. 1906. Oil on cardboard, $25 \times 34''$. *Kimball Art Foundation, Fort Worth*

49. IN THE VICINITY OF CRIQUEBEUF. 1905. Oil on cardboard, $17\frac{3}{4} \times 23\frac{3}{4}''$. *Collection Richard S. Zeisler, New York City*

50. Photograph of Madame Hessel in Vuillard's studio, c. 1905

Denis's dictum that a painting is essentially a flat surface covered with colors arranged in a certain order. Such fascinating experiments demonstrate theory rather than personal predilection, and no matter what he learned from them he never repeated anything like them after he had discovered his own true way—a journey into the mysterious poetic significance of everyday life and of inanimate objects. Its goal was the creation of atmosphere—the Symbolist "air of things"—and the means of reaching it, of course, the intimist style of which Vuillard is the incomparable master.

No artist exists in a vacuum, and the intimist style that Vuillard raised to such high degrees of refinement, with its roots in the Dutch "little masters" and Chardin, was very much in vogue about 1890. Representations of homely subjects, darkish interiors with figures, gardens at dusk, reading by lamplight, children at play, and genre scenes with more feeling than action abounded in Paris galleries. Carrière's studies of maternity, Van Gogh's old shoes, and even Cézanne's solemn cardplayers fit into this category. Vuillard particularly made this style his own in the magical portrayal of what he knew and loved best—his family and his friends.

An air of secrecy envelops Vuillard's intimist pictures. He was well aware of this. Late in life, when showing them publicly for the first time, he exclaimed anxiously, "It's dreadful, revealing all these secrets!" Nothing is openly declared in his oblique approach. We grasp the color pattern before we identify the elusive subject, so disguised is it behind the screen of his deft little dabs of muted color. Nothing happens in these airless paintings, although as we peer into their ambiguous depths we become aware of some imprecise, often urgent meaning that lurks behind the pictorial subtleties. We forget that the figures are doll-like and that the atmosphere of his mother's workshop, where the workers bend over the embroideries, was not intrinsically inspiring. Yet nothing less than the rarest elegance is epitomized in the pose of Madame Vuillard leaning over her stove. No matter how commonplace such subject matter may be, Vuillard transfigures it, weaving diverse, varicolored elements into exquisite compositions whose asymmetry derives from the artifice of Japanese prints. These intimist paintings of the 1890s strike a note of magic that still, in its peculiar muffled way, rings out. They were by no means overlooked by astute contemporaries,

51. LADY IN GRAY. 1905. Oil on canvas, 32 × 26ʹ. *Private collection*

who recognized the originality of their discovery that poetic meaning could be conjured up by the simplest means without recourse to anecdote or drama. Critics also detected the sympathetic links between Vuillard and Symbolist writers. Not for nothing was he identified as a "Verlainian intimist."

Vuillard was not destined to continue painting uninterruptedly these delightful, somewhat claustrophobic interiors which seem to wish to shut the door on the outside world—and keep it shut. Thanks largely to the Natansons' patronage and influence, he undertook during these years a series of large wall decorations for private patrons which exemplify his

gifts at their zenith. The opportunity of painting decorative panels had long been one of Vuillard's ambitions. Nor was he alone in this. A cardinal Nabi doctrine inherited from Gauguin was that all art should be large-scale decoration and not the making of small framed pictures which chopped inspiration into disconnected pieces. Albert Aurier, one of the Nabis' chief literary champions, declared that "painting can only have been created to decorate with thoughts, dreams, and ideas the blank walls of human buildings. The easel picture is nothing but an illogical refinement invented to satisfy the fancy or the commercial spirit of decadent civilizations." He bewailed

52. Pierre Bonnard. STUDY FOR A PORTRAIT OF
EDOUARD VUILLARD. c. 1910. Oil on panel, 18 × 14¾".
Collection Mr. and Mrs. Paul Mellon, Upperville, Virginia

linked rhythmically to the other in flat arabesques.
Color is warm and light and the spirit entirely modern.
As artful illustrations of contemporary life they owe
much to Degas, whose influence on Vuillard was in
the ascendant. Two years later he completed for
Alexandre Natanson a more ambitious series, *Public
Gardens,* enchanting, sunlit outdoor scenes with nurses
and babies and children playing. Their settings suggest the gardens of the Tuileries or the Luxembourg,
and they are Impressionistic in character, indebted
to Monet while remaining entirely personal. In
them, as Claude Roger-Marx perceptively observes,
Vuillard found a happy medium "between Grand
Decoration and easel painting without leaving the
realm of the intimate." From 1896 date the four
panels for Dr. Vaquez's library, tapestry-like interiors
with figures, a riot of shallow pattern-making in the
wallpaper, the shelved books, and the rich dresses
of the women occupied at various useful tasks. Last
of the decorative schemes done in this decade are
the panels painted in 1898 for the novelist Claude
Anet, which depict Misia Natanson's garden at Villeneuve-sur-Yonne in Burgundy. Perhaps the loveliest

the fact that Gauguin, so gifted in decorative painting,
had never had Puvis de Chavannes's mural oppor-
tunities.

By 1890, so the Dutch Nabi Verkade tells us, "the
war cry went up from studio to studio: 'No more
easel pictures! Away with useless bits of furniture!
Painting must not usurp a freedom which cuts it
off from the other arts! The painter's work begins
where the architect decides that his work is finished!
... The wall must be kept as a surface. . . . There
are no such things as pictures, there is only decoration.' " Brave words. But where were the oppor-
tunities? Only Puvis got official commissions.
Nonetheless, Bonnard sent a big composition to the
Indépendants in 1891, while Vuillard began painting
theater sets, a technical and compositional experience
whose importance for him cannot be overemphasized.

Vuillard's first decorative commission—six panels
and a screen executed for Paul Desmarais in 1892—
relates closely to his intimism with its frieze of women
sewing, gardening, petting dogs, walking about, each

53. Photograph of La Place Vintimille, 1911

54. LA PLACE VINTIMILLE (two panels). c. 1908. Distemper on board, mounted on canvas, $76 \times 25\frac{1}{2}$" each.
Collection J. K. Thannhauser, New York City. Courtesy of Thannhauser Foundation

of all, in subtlety, intricacy, suppressed feeling, lyricism of color, and beauty of touch, they are irresistible.

When he first saw some of these panels in 1905, André Gide was struck by their beauty. His words are worth quoting as they apply to Vuillard's work as a whole. " To return to M. Vuillard's decorations," he wrote, "I don't know quite what is the most admirable thing about them. Perhaps it is M. Vuillard himself. He is the most personal, the most intimate of story-tellers. I know few pictures which bring the observer so directly into conversation with the artist. I think it must be because his brush never breaks free of the motion which guides it; the outer world, for Vuillard, is always a pretext, an adjustable means of expression. And above all it's because M. Vuillard speaks almost in a whisper—as is only right when confidences are being exchanged—and we have to bend over towards him to hear what he says."

"There is nothing sentimental," continues Gide, "or high-falutin' about the discreet melancholy which pervades his work. Its dress is that of everyday. It is tender, and caressing; and if it were not for the mastery that already marks it, I should call it timid. For all his success, I can sense in Vuillard the charm of anxiety and doubt. He never brings forward a color without making it possible for it to fall back, subtly and delightfully, into the background. Too fastidious for plain statement, he proceeds by insinuation. . . . He never strives for brilliant effect; harmony of tone is his continual preoccupation; science and intuition play a double role in the disposition of his colors, and each one of them casts new light on its neighbor, and as it were exacts a confession from it."

Long before the end of the 1890s the Nabis had disbanded as a close-knit intellectual group. After the first excitement of Gauguin had reaped its harvest for them, their relations were based on friendship rather than on common aesthetic grounds. Vuillard soon lost what little interest he had ever had in artists who tried to turn picture-making into formulas. He and Bonnard, with whom he remained on intimate terms, no longer wished to abolish Impressionism. In fact, they sought to refine it. Vuillard reached artistic

55. STREETS OF PARIS (four panels). c. 1908. Distemper on canvas, 74½ × 17″ each. *Private collection, New York City*

56. SCENE FROM MOLIÈRE'S "LE MALADE IMAGINAIRE." 1913. Distemper on canvas, 71 × 118″.
Propriété de la Société Immobilière du Théâtre des Champs-Elysées. Foyer de la Comédie des Champs-Elysées

57. SCENE FROM TRISTAN BERNARD'S "LE PETIT CAFÉ." 1913. Distemper on canvas, 71 × 110¼″.
Propriété de la Société Immobilière du Théâtre des Champs-Elysées. Foyer de la Comédie des Champs-Elysées

maturity by intuitive and empirical ways, not by way of theory.

During the years of the big decorations, Vuillard continued to paint his dusky little interiors, allusive impressionistic slices of life. Many of them were done on cardboard, a method he probably learned from Lautrec, who figured prominently in the Natanson circle. Vuillard often exhibited at the gallery of Le Barc de Boutteville and, in 1897–98, at that of the famous Ambroise Vollard, who encouraged Vuillard's printmaking and in 1899 published his most important series of color lithographs, *Paysages et Intérieurs*. So far, success had come to Vuillard only in his confined and private world, but this was to change shortly. An enlargement of his entire way of life was largely due to the activity of the art gallery Bernheim-Jeune, and its director, Jos Hessel. From 1900 until 1940 the Hessels, particularly Madame Hessel, were to dominate almost all aspects of Vuillard's life.

Jos Hessel was one of the first art dealers of a kind that is familiar today: he sought out gifted contemporaries, found patrons and commissions for them, and looked after their interests in general. Before that time artists had to try to sell work themselves or else hire public places in which to show it. The new system enormously benefited Vuillard, ridding him of all financial and merchandising responsibilities. As an impresario, Hessel was energetic and resourceful and made himself indispensable. Shortly after 1900 Vuillard and the Hessels became inseparable, spending almost every evening together in the Hessels' Paris apartment. During the summer Vuillard traveled or went to Brittany and Normandy with them, and in later years he became a semipermanent guest at their country houses on the outskirts of Paris.

This was all very well and allowed his life to run smoothly and even luxuriously. But Vuillard was notably unworldly, and it is surprising that he so willingly settled into the alien Hessel world—a rich and somewhat vulgar segment of the bourgeoisie made up of stockbrokers, theater people, publishers, writers, and successful professional men. He cut a strange and aloof figure at the Hessels' boisterous gatherings; indeed, Vuillard would usually steal away with a book after greeting the guests with a modesty and courtesy that impressed everyone. Some thought he secretly nourished rebellious thoughts in this

58. PORTRAIT OF MISIA. 1914. Distemper and charcoal on cardboard, 17×14⅜". *The Museum of Modern Art, New York City. Gift of Mr. and Mrs. Eli Wallach*

59. CHAPEL OF VERSAILLES. 1918. Distemper on paper, mounted on canvas, 37¾×26". *Collection Jacques Laroche, Beaulieu-sur-Mer*

60. CARD PARTY AT VAUCRESSON. 1920–22. Oil on paper, 39½ × 30″. *Private collection, Paris*

61. LA SALLE DES CARYATIDES, LOUVRE. 1921. Distemper on canvas, 63 × 51⅛″. *Bauer-Judlin Collection, Basel*

gilded cage from which, however, he never broke free. The explanation lies in his almost lover-like relationship with Madame Hessel, known as his "dragon"—a vital, handsome woman, much taller than Vuillard, and thoroughly devoted to him. She can readily be recognized as a mother-figure, and Madame Vuillard is said to have been jealous of her. She was the second woman in his life, and he painted her almost as often as he did the first.

On a more exalted social level stood the salon of Princesse Hélène Bibesco, where a galaxy of intellectuals, musicians, and aristocrats assembled. It was there that Vuillard met her two sons, Emmanuel and Antoine. And there he also met Marcel Proust. A souvenir of their friendship, apparently now lost, once existed. One evening in the summer of 1902, when Antoine and his friends were dining at Armenonville in the Bois de Boulogne, Vuillard made a sketch of the party—"a unique point of intersection between his admirable talent, which has so often kindled my memory, and one of the most delightful and perfect hours of my life," as Proust wrote in a request to buy the sketch.

Another meeting between Vuillard and Proust took place at Cabourg in the summer of 1907. As one of the few verbatim accounts of Vuillard it deserves quoting, particularly in view of its inevitable sequel. Calling one day at Vuillard's studio he found him, as he wrote Reynaldo Hahn, dressed in blue overalls, "of rather too pastel shade, I thought." Vuillard held forth on the subject of painting: "A chap like Giotto, d'you see, or then a chap like Titian, knew every bit as much as Monet, or then again, a chap like Raphael, d'you see. . . ." So on and so forth. "He's no ordinary man, even if he does say 'chap' every twenty seconds," Proust concluded. Never one to waste an opportunity, he recalled these remarks when constructing the character of Elstir, the Impressionist painter in *Remembrance of Things Past*. In the novel Proust has Elstir comment on the sculpture in the church at Balbec in much the same way: "The chap who carved that facade of yours," says Elstir, "was every bit as fine a fellow, you can take it from me, as the people you admire most nowadays." Such remarks probably reflect, faithfully enough, Vuillard's increasing conservatism after 1900 and his dissociation from the avant-garde of the generation after his own.

Vuillard can be compared with Proust in several ways, for example in his use of the action of memory

62. Left: SALLE LA CAZE, LOUVRE. 1921. Distemper on canvas, $63 \times 51\frac{1}{8}''$. *Bauer-Judlin Collection, Basel*

63. MADAME VUILLARD, LE MATIN, RUE DE CALAIS. c. 1922. Oil on millboard, $17\frac{1}{8} \times 11\frac{3}{4}''$. *Collection Mr. and Mrs. Paul Mellon, Upperville, Virginia*

64. STUDY FOR PORTRAIT OF MAURICE DENIS. 1925. Distemper on paper, $44 \times 54''$. *Musée du Petit-Palais, Paris*

41

to embellish, and occasionally transform, a theme. We are told that he would make numerous sketches of a subject and from them—rather than directly from the subject—elaborate a final, almost visionary version of the facts and thereby discover what one might call their spiritual equivalent. On the other hand, again like Proust, he would in his portraits turn a rich and meticulously handled setting into an extension of a sitter's personality. According to Claude Roger-Marx, the *Nouvelle Revue Française* hoped that Vuillard would illustrate *Swann's Way*. He remarks, "What hand could better have expressed the world of Proust?"

This brings us to Vuillard's late portraiture, of which more than forty major examples date from after 1920. To the social historian they are of considerable fascination. As period documents they shed valuable light on costume, interior decoration, and on the way of life of the French high bourgeoisie during the two closing decades of the Third Republic. Furthermore, many of them portray persons of some eminence: artists such as Bonnard, Maillol, Forain, Denis, and Roussel; the Comtesse de Noailles, Jean Giraudoux, and Paul Léautaud among writers; the politician Philippe Berthelot; the actresses Yvonne Printemps and Jane Renouart, as well as other outstanding figures of the day. Their interest is un-

65. MADAME TRISTAN BERNARD IN HER LIVING ROOM. 1925. Oil on canvas, 11½ × 14". *Collection Mr. and Mrs. Alex M. Lewyt, New York*

66. The last photograph of Vuillard's mother, about 1926

deniable and they are on the whole well painted.

Why then should they present such a stumbling block to Vuillard's admirers? Why did they cause his critics to write him off as a painter who had nothing left but taste and honesty of vision, a no-more-than-competent academic artist? Critics explain the withering of his imagination by arguing that he found himself out of his depth in rich bourgeois society; that he could only do justice to people and scenes he knew profoundly; and that his famous intimism ill suited fashionable sitters to whom he was mostly indifferent. Vuillard was fond of saying, "I don't paint portraits. I paint people in their homes." This remark can be turned against him by observing that in some of his most highly finished portraits he gives sitters little more importance than their surroundings. In short, trivial accessories threaten to overwhelm them. Furthermore, he lacked the analytical and satirical powers of a Jacques-Emile Blanche, a lesser artist but better portraitist. He stopped short of seeing through conventional appearance. Hence the blandness of these expert performances where imagination fails to take high flights. Nonetheless, these portraits, the results of prolonged observation, are rooted in veracity. Each is unique in representation, not in any way dependent on a formula. What we miss in their relentless objectivity is the painter's personality.

67. MADAME VUILLARD. c. 1926. Charcoal, $23\frac{3}{4} \times 29\frac{1}{8}''$. *Private collection, Paris*

68. PORTRAIT OF MADAME BÉNARD. c. 1927–30. Distemper on canvas, $44\frac{1}{8} \times 39\frac{3}{4}''$. *Musée National d'Art Moderne, Paris*

69. STUDY FOR PORTRAIT OF
LA COMTESSE DE NOAILLES.
c. 1932. Charcoal on canvas, 43¼×50⅜".
Musée National d'Art Moderne, Paris

70. A MEETING AT THE INSTITUTE. 1937. Distemper on paper, mounted on canvas, 39⅜×29⅛". *Private
collection, Paris*

Until he painted the late rather fashionable portraits,
Vuillard's art had escaped an encounter with life's
grosser realities. In the beginning the particular associations he evoked were in tune with his own. But
when strangers simply "posed," he had to sacrifice too
much in order to record worldly display, a role
which wasted his marvelous facility. The elements
of positive sympathy and artist-sitter rapport are indispensable ingredients in portraiture that only inter-
mittently appear in Vuillard's work of the 1920s.
Quick and competent perception is one thing, brood-
ing reflection another.

Portraiture by no means wholly occupied Vuillard's
mature years. From 1900 on, his decorative work
comes increasingly to terms with the visual world,
taking a more expansive, detached view of it. No
more dusky, humble interiors and figures wrapped
in poetic ambiguity. The painter moves from his
stifling rooms to the outdoors, to the sun-drenched
garden where we smell the newly watered flowers,
and to the beach where we breathe the air from the
sea. Interiors are now sumptuous and brilliantly
lighted, and a pearly, silvery haze drapes his magical
views of Paris. Color takes on a new refulgence and

Vuillard, Symbolism behind him, becomes a late if not the last Impressionist.

Although permanently established in Paris, moving in 1907 to a flat overlooking the Place Vintimille which he shared with his mother, Vuillard was not in later life a wholly sedentary person. He traveled in Spain with Bonnard and the Bibesco brothers in 1905; he went to Germany in 1913; and he was constantly taking trips with the Hessels in addition to spending summers with them and virtually living with them after his mother's death in 1928. But Vuillard was always happy to return to Paris and to his studio. "The painter's instrument," he would say, "is his armchair." Major late commissions include murals for the Palais de Chaillot and for the League of Nations in Geneva. In 1937 he became a member of the Institut de France. Remembering his earlier refusal of the Legion of Honor, this acceptance caused some surprise. But his friends insisted, and he probably saw no more in it than an opportunity of being useful. The German invasion of 1940 dealt a decisive blow to his declining health. Friends persuaded him to leave Paris just before the collapse of the Third Republic, to whose way of life at its happiest he had borne such eloquent testimony. He died in Brittany, by the sea at La Baule, on June 21, 1940. It was time. Never demonstrative about it, patriotism ran deep in his nature.

After his death the work of an artist continues a life of its own, either expanding or contracting in the emotional climate of succeeding generations. Vuillard's has certainly expanded, although its tranquility and sense of static happiness may not be emotions indulged in today. His art, so faithful to the conventions and beliefs of his age, still reaches out vitally from the past. It combines simplicity of utterance with complete aesthetic mastery. Vuillard remains one of our conquerors. He illuminated, transformed, and enchanted the usual and in this field stands supreme.

Perhaps Vuillard's best epitaph was provided in the poetic tribute paid him by his friend the distinguished playwright Jean Giraudoux, who wrote that "all of nature willingly accepts, since Vuillard is dead, to be seen by everyone as she was seen by him. Today she delights to give to everyone, in homage to Vuillard dead and Vuillard resurrected, what alone was owing to Vuillard, and makes the whole of France his pastel and his crown."

71. LA COMÉDIE. 1937. Oil on canvas, 20⅞ × 21⅝″. *Private collection, Paris*

72. PORTRAIT OF ELVIRA POPESCO. 1938. Oil on canvas, 40 × 32″. *Mr. and Mrs. Josef Rosensaft, New York City*

73. SELF-PORTRAIT. 1925. Distemper on cardboard, 32 × 26½″. *Collection Ian Woodner, New York City*

COLORPLATES

Painted 1891

PORTRAIT OF LUGNÉ-POË

Oil on panel, 8 ³/₄ × 10 ¹/₄″

Collection Fletcher Steele, Pittsford, New York

Few persons were more fortunate than Vuillard in his friends, who, as one of them wrote, "opened and closed his horizons." Utterly devoted to him, they constantly stood at hand to cheer him when his spirits faltered, to urge him forward when diffidence held him back, or simply to find commissions for him or sell his pictures. Vuillard needed dynamic impresarios and never failed to find them. Outstanding among his earlier champions was Lugné-Poë (1869–1940), actor, producer, and director (1893) of the Théâtre de l'Oeuvre, which largely introduced the work of foreign playwrights to French audiences and encouraged new dramatists as well as new forms of dramatic art and production. Lugné had been Vuillard's schoolmate at the Lycée Condorcet and shared a studio with him in 1891 when this witty portrait was painted. In it Vuillard applies Nabi aesthetic principles with extreme rigor: deep space is nonexistent; areas of strong, flat color obey a pronounced rhythmic pattern bearing little more than a decorative relationship to the contours of the sitter; and the portrait symbolizes Lugné's intense youthful drive rather than portraying him literally. He must have been a formidable young man, both "querulous and fierce," as André Gide described him, "someone who gave the impression that his foot had just been trodden upon."

Painted 1892

LILACS

Oil on cardboard, 14 × 11¹/₈″
Collection Mr. and Mrs. Donald S. Stralem, New York City

Signifying the drastic nature of Vuillard's break with academic art, this glorious outburst of youthful genius can almost be regarded as a perfect demonstration of Nabi techniques and of their way of re-creating the visual world. The group believed that appearances should not be reproduced in a literal manner; that color should be laid on in semiarbitrary flat patches; and that nature could and should permissibly be deformed in the search for an ideal of decorative beauty. Vuillard's bold simplifications here of flowers, leaves, and vase follow these precepts to the letter, and the results, judged by any standards, are striking, original, fresh, and fascinating. As part of Vuillard's total oeuvre, paintings adhering strictly to Nabi theory represent no more than a brief moment in his precocious development. The quality and conviction of paintings of this period clearly indicate that for a short time Vuillard must have been convinced of these ideas, but in the long run it ran against his grain to paint a picture, such as this one, according to a formula. In conversation he dismissed Gauguin, who was responsible for the formula, as a "pedant." His own sensibilities could not help breaking through theory.

Painted about 1892–93

WOMAN SWEEPING IN A ROOM

Oil on cardboard, 18 × 19"
The Phillips Collection, Washington, D.C.

Vuillard's intimist interiors of the 1890s, of which this is an outstandingly beautiful example, immediately suggest their descent from Chardin to whom, in truth, they owe much. In short, this scene of everyday domestic tranquility belongs, for its invincible humanity and for its uniformly rich paint texture, at the heart of the French genre tradition. What Marcel Proust wrote about Chardin applies here as well. "The pleasure you get," he wrote, "from his painting of a room where a woman sits sewing . . . is the pleasure —seized on the wing, redeemed from the transient, ascertained, pondered, perpetuated—that he got from the sight of a room where a woman sat sewing. . . . You already experienced it subconsciously, this pleasure one gets from everyday scenes and inanimate objects, otherwise it would not have arisen in your heart when Chardin summoned it in his ringing, commanding accents." There are Dutch influences here too, perhaps reminiscences of Vermeer in the geometrical lucidity of the surface organization (no arabesques, for once). A reminder of the exoticism of Japanese art, which fascinated Vuillard's whole generation, might be found in the presence of that sumptuous lacquered Oriental jar perched so unexpectedly atop the plain chest of drawers. How comprehensibly Vuillard pulls all the disparate elements together. We look at a tenderly poetized interior and, simultaneously, at a magical pattern of intricate harmonies.

Painted 1893

INTERIOR

Oil on cardboard, 12 $^1/_2$ × 14 $^3/_8$″
Smith College Museum of Art, Northampton, Massachusetts

The traditional title of this delightful painting, *Interior at l'Etang-la-Ville,* is invalidated by the date of its conception, seven years before Roussel and his family moved to that suburb of Paris. It does represent the interior of Madame Vuillard's workroom in the Rue St. Honoré, and has for its principal characters Vuillard's elder sister Marie, busy sorting materials, and his great friend the painter Ker-Xavier Roussel, who shyly peeps around the flowered screen at the young woman. In fact their marriage took place in 1893, so the painting constitutes a sort of pictorial epithalamium, a celebration of the Vuillard family happiness at this event. So few of Vuillard's interiors have any dramatic content that this little scene, with its faintly theatrical air, stands out exceptionally. How subtly the two main characters, mutually watchful, relate one to the other. Vuillard's training in the theater was not wasted. As a work of art it cannot be better described than in the words written that same year about Vuillard's interiors by the critic Gustave Geffroy: "His paintings remind me of the obverse of a tapestry; the weight of the human figures, and the gold and silver of light, and the velvet of shadow—all appear in different guise. His is an art, too, of attitudes, and folded arms, and pale hands. Vuillard has found a new and delicious way of expressing the poetry of a quiet hearth and the beauty of thought and action that underlies that poetry."

Painted about 1893

MOTHER AND SISTER
OF THE ARTIST

Oil on canvas, 18 ¹/₄ × 22 ¹/₄"

The Museum of Modern Art, New York City. Gift of Mrs. Saidie A. May

One wonders just what Vuillard's contemporaries thought of such a revolutionary kind of interior with figures as this one, so ingenious, deliberate, and, for all its whimsicality, so in touch with reality. The answer is that they saw the point and were impressed. "Vuillard is a painter," wrote the critic Gustave Geffroy in 1893, "whose understanding gives me great delight. He accentuates his vision of the world; he penetrates the whole of life; he looks closely at those aspects of it which it pleases him to evoke. . . . It is furniture that he cares for, and carpets, and a fine bed-cover, and the ordinary equipment of the table; and the stuffs of which inexpensive dresses are made—dark, it may be, or brightly colored, or striped, or spotted like a guinea-fowl's feathers." To his natural intimist sensitivity Vuillard added influences from without. The contorted pose of his sister Marie, pushing herself away from the wall to avoid being absorbed into the conflict of pronounced patterns, can be attributed to Japanese prints, and the artifice of the whole composition, perhaps to his work in the theater. One feels that the couple is "on stage." And certainly Vuillard's early years spent in and about his mother's workroom sharpened his eye for small things, for colors, materials, patterns, and for human oddities.

KER-XAVIER ROUSSEL
READING A NEWSPAPER

Oil on cardboard, 9 × 11"
Private collection, Paris

Probably painted a year after Roussel's marriage to Vuillard's sister, this vivid little likeness, so rooted in the intimate affection between artist and sitter, allows the latter's personality to determine the structure and character of the picture. Taught by Degas, whose influence predominates here, to catch figures rapidly in a momentary pose, Vuillard makes a succinct, informal portrait statement. Indeed, it is difficult to believe that Roussel is actually posing; rather, he seems to have been caught unawares. Yet how artful is the simplicity of this solid design in which capricious details, such as the cut-off left foot and the mysterious swag of material in the upper right corner, repay Vuillard's debt to Japanese prints, whose audacities stimulated so many French progressive artists, especially after the Japanese exhibition at the Ecole des Beaux-Arts in 1890.

Painted 1894

THE PARK

Distemper on canvas, 83 × 62 ³/₄"

Collection Mr. and Mrs. William B. Jaffe, New York City

For many persons the big decorations evoking the parks and gardens of Paris executed during the 1890s occupy a supreme place in Vuillard's work. He was never more of a Nabi than in creating them. For one of the Nabis' fundamental beliefs held that all art is decoration. "Painting," wrote Albert Aurier, one of their literary champions, "can only have been created to decorate with thoughts, dreams, and ideas the blank walls of human buildings." This sparkling panel that once belonged to Thadée Natanson ideally exemplifies Vuillard's interpretation of that belief. Claude Roger-Marx describes it in a characteristically discerning manner: "We see a servant in a light-coloured apron and a striped jacket, in charge of a group of children. The vista, slightly broadening downwards, allows us to see the other people ranged in depth in the background. The cream-coloured patina of the tall houses, with their vertical rows of balconies and shutters, is described through breaks in the foliage. These buildings remind us that parks and squares of Paris are just artificial oases or imitation woodland bordered by masonry. The right of the composition is held by the main group, made up by a baby in a tartan dress sprawling on the ground, a little girl in a black pinafore standing, and two small boys struggling; on the left, the gravelled path winds upwards, growing narrower towards the centre. At that point a bearded promenader wearing a Panama hat bends over a seated lady. Behind them, mothers and children, a variegated mass, animate the summer shade. Tender greens mix with darker greens and blues, modulation and correspondance is the rule. The splaying slats of a bench contrast with the stripes on a bodice and the dots on a skirt. No Japanese print is more subtly matt." There is an ineffable charm here for which the perfectly ordinary elements of the scene can hardly account. As so often in his work, Vuillard turns the commonplace into a vision of serenity and enchantment.

Three panels from the series PUBLIC GARDENS Painted 1894

LEFT TO RIGHT:

CHILDREN PLAYING AND NURSES
$84^1/_2 \times 28^3/_8''$

THREE WOMEN ON A BENCH
$84^1/_2 \times 59^7/_8''$.

WOMAN IN BLACK SEATED ON A BENCH
$84^1/_2 \times 31^1/_2''$

Distemper on canvas

Musée National d'Art Moderne, Paris

Vuillard's first major scheme of decorations for residential interiors was executed for the Paul Desmarais family, cousins of the Natansons, in 1892. The Desmarais decorations were followed two years later by a more ambitious undertaking on nine panels, *Public Gardens,* commissioned from the young artist by Alexandre Natanson, Thadée's older brother, for the dining room of his apartment at 60 Avenue du Bois de Boulogne (now Avenue Foch). There they remained until their dispersal at auction in 1929, when three major panels were acquired by the French government, and two of the remaining six came to private collections in this country. These five panels are illustrated in this book. The series depicts, with considerable cunning and artifice, everyday scenes inspired by the Tuileries and Luxembourg gardens, or by the Bois de Boulogne. Here children play, looked after by watchful nurses; older people sun themselves on benches, or stroll about under parasols. Sunlight flecks the patches of warm gravel, illuminates the cool metallic greens of the massed foliage and the curtain of clipped and squared trees now and then opening out onto the pale sky. In these and other delightful decorations Vuillard moves out of doors without leaving the realm of the intimate.

It has often been noticed, and correctly, that Vuillard combines here the open-air feeling of Monet's Impressionism with the grand decorative manner of Puvis de Chavannes's stately and pondered compositions where nothing is left to chance, not even the calculated role played by the intervals of open space between each carefully posed figure. Nor did Vuillard forget that these panels were destined to decorate and reinforce the intimacy of a bourgeois interior of modest proportions, not a public building. Hence they are far less gravè than Puvis's majestic compositions, and hence the imposed flatness of the designs; the greenery prevents deep space from making a hole in the walls of a room. The artist strikes the most cheerful notes of a wonderful morning in springtime Paris. And he recovers for us an imaginary age of innocence.

One incidental story is told about the party given by the Natansons to show these new decorations to their friends. Vuillard was naturally a center of attention, and Toulouse-Lautrec, misguidedly attempting to enliven the affair, gave him some kind of strong mixed drink, obviously an early form of the cocktail. The next thing that Vuillard, normally the most abstemious of men, knew was his awakening the next morning, fully clothed, in a Natanson guest room. Such were some of the pranks in the *Revue Blanche* circle.

Panel from the series PUBLIC GARDENS

Painted 1894

UNDER THE TREES

Distemper on canvas, 84¹/₂ × 38¹/₂"
The Cleveland Museum of Art. Gift of the Hanna Fund

Although no single panel of the nine originally composing *Public Gardens* is less than enchanting and unable to stand by itself, it is unfortunate that the ensemble was broken up and dispersed throughout the world. For these panels were intended to be seen together as a single related decorative scheme for a particular room. This kind of wall decoration, where paintings in series were adapted to architecture, was a revival on the part of the Nabis of an older French tradition rarely practiced by artists since the eighteenth century. One thinks of rooms decorated by painters such as Boucher and Fragonard. With some notable exceptions, such as Delacroix, nineteenth-century painters preferred to consider themselves individualists, creating works of art that were in no way subservient to clients' wishes or to architectural demands. The Nabis, on the other hand, delighted in being thought of as decorative artists who would turn their talents willingly to a variety of mediums such as stained glass, tapestry, screens, theater sets, and the like. In this way they formed unusually close ties with enlightened patrons like members of the Natanson family.

It appears that Odilon Redon largely encouraged them in these diversified tasks, advising them to study Delacroix's murals in the Louvre and elsewhere in order to discover the secrets of decorative painting. Naturally each Nabi followed his own bent. As has already been mentioned, it is fairly obvious that Vuillard's tutelary dieties in *Public Gardens* were Monet and Puvis de Chavannes. From the former he learned the use of light colors, how to look intently at nature in full sunlight, and register its phenomena joyfully; thus he succeeded in prolonging the optimism and serenity of Impressionism. From the latter he learned how to impose a formal, flat pattern on what the eye saw, leading to a slightly artificial interpretation of the contemporary scene that created a pronounced aesthetic flavor rather than a mere facsimile.

Panel from the series PUBLIC GARDENS

Painted 1894

PROMENADE

Distemper on canvas, 84¹/₂ × 38¹/₂"
The Museum of Fine Arts, Houston. Robert Lee Blaffer Memorial Collection

As are the other panels of the Natanson series, this idyllic scene of children playing in a park under a cloudless sky is painted in distemper, a medium in which powdered colors are mixed with glue and water without the addition of oil. Although not widely employed by artists, it has the merits of being easy to handle, relatively cheap, and extremely permanent. "A splendid material," wrote one expert in the field. "For atmosphere unequalled, and for strength as powerful as oil, in half an hour you can do with it that which in water or oil would take one or two days." Distemper, or *colle* as it is referred to in French, is particularly used by scene and poster painters and found special favor with Vuillard, who learned the technique in the early 1890s when he was painting theater sets for Lugné-Poë's Théâtre de l'Oeuvre. Unfortunately the sets have long since been destroyed, but what he discovered during their execution remained for long years in his art. Distemper suited Vuillard's painting temperament, and he used it for almost every large painting he ever made. The colors dried fast, facilitating constant retouching by means of which a subject would mature to its final state under the guidance of his precise and detailed memory. The continuing freshness of Vuillard's pictures done in this medium, which he often combined with gouache and pastel, testifies to his technical abilities and knowledge of what suited him best.

Painted 1896

INTERIOR WITH FIGURE

Oil on canvas, 19 ¹/₂ × 20 ³/₄"
The Robert Lehman Collection, New York City

In very few of Vuillard's intimist interiors of his mother sitting in a room does he express so triumphantly the full density and complexity of real things. And few are as mutely or richly stated as this small oil, formed out of a multitude of tiny touches into an impressive whole, much like the patient construction of a coral reef. The artist achieves this miraculous result much in the manner of his admired Chardin who, in the words of Marcel Proust, combined "things and people in those rooms which are more than a thing and perhaps more than a person, rooms which are the scene of their joint lives, the law of their affinities or contrarieties, the pervasive secreted scent of their charm, the confidant, mute yet a blabber, of their soul, the shrine of their past. As befits people and things who have lived quietly together for a long time, either needing the other, and finding an obscure pleasure as well in each other's company, everything in such a room breathes friendship." Our first visual impression is of an interplay of tone and color, explicit yet mysterious. We feel it, but how can we begin to describe, much less to analyze, the mutations of this warm interplay. How bold are the patterned tablecloth and the red curtains; how subtle the golden haze of sunlight lingering on the walls, the ceiling, and on the bent figure sewing by the window. Like Chardin, Vuillard makes us believe in the unnoticed life of inanimate objects. And like a Mallarmé poem, we are in the world of nuance and allusion so very much a part of fin-de-siècle Paris.

Painted about 1897

MISIA AND THADÉE NATANSON

Oil on paper mounted on canvas, 41 × 28"

The Museum of Modern Art, New York City. Gift of Nate B. and Frances Spingold

This delicate and rapturous double portrait of Vuillard's cherished friends and early supporters represents his feeling at its warmest, as well as at its most private and civilized. The setting, aglow with golden evening light, is the drawing room of the Natansons' Paris apartment in the Rue St. Florentin where the artist, not a little bit under the spell of Misia's siren charms, spent many happy hours. It would be hard to find a more intensely personal expression of the emotion that Misia aroused in him and of the ties that bound him to her. So strong and vivid was her personality, and so overwhelming its effects on Vuillard, that by contrast Thadée, leaning over the piano in the background, is reduced to a depersonalized colored shape whose identity is almost lost against the lively pattern of the wallpaper. That Misia is evidently listening to music is conveyed not so much by the presence of the piano as by her rapt contemplative air and by the inward expression on her beautiful face with its closed eyes. Music played a great part in Misia's life, both before and after her marriage to Thadée Natanson, founder, in 1891, of the *Revue Blanche*, the outstanding literary review in the Paris of its day. The magazine was often illustrated by lithographs by Vuillard and other avant-garde artists of the period. Born of Polish extraction in St. Petersburg in 1872, Misia studied music with Fauré and developed into a brilliant pianist before going on to become one of the queens of Paris between 1900 and 1940. But in the 1890s her circle was literary and artistic. The poets Mallarmé and Verlaine were among her admirers, and she held a court of intellectuals, both in Paris and in the country, from which Vuillard was seldom absent. Quite rightly she described herself as a "muse."

Painted 1897

ROOM UNDER THE EAVES

Oil on cardboard, 18 × 25 ³/₄"

Collection Mr. and Mrs. B. E. Bensinger, Chicago

Who else but Misia Natanson could have inspired Vuillard to the degree of delicate and passionate comprehension of this ultrapoetic mysterious interior. And, indeed, here she is, faintly lamp-lighted, seated at a table with Thadée in an upper room of their country house at Villeneuve-sur-Yonne. Vuillard spent much of the summer of 1897 with them, and as an imaginative interpretation of a scene it distills the quintessence of Symbolist intimism, combining a pitch of feeling and a pure aesthetic pleasure arising from, rather than bounded by, a given visual scene. This quiet painting represents a unique and private vision of the artist's world. Vuillard found here an experience more vivid than anything his eyes merely saw. The dark was light enough. Nonetheless, painting depends on visual data as well as on ideas, and the more we look into this magical evening interior the more we see of it—the criss-crossing rafters, the dusky blue ceiling, the red brocaded chair, the ghostly bunch of flowers, and, of course, the piano, never far from Misia, who will perhaps soon sit down at it to dash off some Chopin in her fiery Polish manner.

AUX TUILERIES

Oil on panel, 15 ¹/₄ × 13"
Collection Mr. and Mrs. Paul Mellon, Upperville, Virginia

Vuillard never tired of painting intimist outdoor scenes such as this corner of the Tuileries gardens not far from the Rue St. Honoré, where he was living at the end of the 1890s. It is related to the Natanson decorations of these years, although less contrived, more informal, and more true to a specific place. In fact, we know just where we are and can easily recognize the windows, with their striped awnings, of the buildings in the Rue de Rivoli looking out over the marshalled trees and the alleys and terraces. The painting's charm is palpable and one succumbs to it without difficulty; it breathes an air of immemorial serenity. Much has changed in the world during the past three-quarters of a century, but this scene remains basically as it was, still populated by children, strollers, and people sunning themselves as they respond gratefully to the warmth and geniality of a felicitous Paris morning in spring. The Nabi spirit still lingers in the slightly theatrical artifice of this scene. Vuillard's more expansive Impressionist period still lay ahead.

Painted 1898

WOMAN SEATED IN A GARDEN

Distemper on canvas, 84 $^1/_2$ × 63 $^3/_8$″
Collection James Dugdale, Crathorne, England

Perhaps the most enchanting of all Vuillard's decorations are the two panels (one of which is illustrated here) painted for the novelist Claude Anet and later, for many years, owned by the artist's close friend Prince Antoine Bibesco. Actually a third panel for this scheme once existed, but it was cut in two and totally repainted by Vuillard at the end of his life. More personal than *Public Gardens*, depicting as they do actual scenes and people cherished by the artist, the twin panels express his deepest private feelings. The setting for these outdoor idylls, so cunningly composed with arabesques of receding shapes and an interplay of warm and cool color, is Thadée Natanson's country house at Villeneuve-sur-Yonne where Vuillard spent so much time around the turn of the century, more or less under Misia Natanson's spell. Here Misia languishes seductively in the foreground of a perfect rural scene that winds gently back from the peopled garden to the distant Burgundian uplands that rise cloud-shadowed against the richly condensed horizon. There is a unified fluency here, which stems from the artist's gazing intently at people and objects and then performing rhapsodic variations on a visual theme. Line, color, and texture all contribute to the vividness of the scene where emotion is so intermixed with pictorial felicities that we can hardly tell whether the scene is more deeply felt than represented.

Painted 1898

WOMAN
READING IN A GARDEN

Distemper on canvas, 84 $^1/_2$ × 63 $^3/_8$"
Collection James Dugdale, Crathorne, England

The companion panel to that of Misia relaxing under the trees (previous page) presents another view of the Natanson garden, showing a corner of the unpretentious house whose windows are shuttered tight against the midday glare. Some people wander idly in the middle distance while, prominent in the foreground, seated on a bench, are Pierre Bonnard and Marthe, his companion since the early 1890s and his future wife. The scene is ordinary—even banal—with no overt emotional appeal, merely depicting a young woman reading a magazine while her bearded companion leans over to play with a kitten. Yet in their casual disregard of one another, and in their relaxed proximity, we can sense the existence of a close, strong relationship between them. This pastoral symphony illustrates very well Vuillard's method of painting wall decorations. Despite the diminishing scale of the background figures the overriding impression is one of flatness. Rich color luxuriates—greens, ochers, reds, pinks, lilacs, among which the sharp blacks and whites ring out dominatingly. "All sorts of contradictions," writes Claude Roger-Marx, "are skilfully upheld . . . the people appear to be composed of the same substance as the landscape; the path is the same color as the flesh; a cloud is puffed out like a dress; a fabric looks like a field; what seems to be a butterfly is a passer-by."

In these pictorial hymns to nature and to love, Vuillard transports us into a realm of pure poetry whose elements, although rooted in reality, are intensified, spiritualized, almost transfigured. The dreamlike character of the Anet panels, more suggested than stated, is profoundly Symbolist. We have portrayed here, as has been finely said, not so much the happiness of living in a beautiful garden as the happiness of thinking about a beautiful garden where one might live. It is the memory of a vision, not the vision itself. Its charm enthralls us as the reflection or echo of an exquisite moment.

Painted 1898

STILL LIFE WITH THE ARTIST'S PAINT BOX AND MOSS ROSES

Oil on canvas, 14 × 16¹/₂"
Estate of Ailsa Mellon Bruce

Still life as a valid subject for a painting originated in the Netherlands, where artists delighted in depicting the abundance of good things available to the taste and appetite of a rich bourgeoisie. As an art form it was later refined by the French, notably by Chardin, who did not treat it merely decoratively but as a noble, self-sufficient theme. At the end of the nineteenth century Odilon Redon raised this genre to a new pitch of refinement, even lending mystical poetic meaning to his flower subjects. Vuillard, who knew and admired the older man, was undoubtedly influenced by him in the still lifes he painted around 1900. But, unlike Redon, he did not attach spiritual significance to flower subjects. With exquisite taste in color and design he gave them an objective, accurate rendering carried out with uniform and loving sympathy.

Painted about 1898

ROOM WITH THREE LAMPS

Distemper on canvas, 22 ⁷/₈ × 37"
Collection Gustave Zumsteg, Zurich

This interior, of subdued splendor, represents the salon of Misia Natanson in the Rue St. Florentin. It is a room of charming proportions where the lamps, shedding a dim but genial light, play on the vaguely established figures, the bursts of greenery, the rectangles of soft color, and the rich tapestry. The whole scene is gentle, melancholy, and sweet, full of revelations and of dignified intervals. In a marked way the picture is suffused with the esoteric work of the writer Mallarmé, spirit of Symbolist poetry and friend of both Misia and Vuillard. "To suggest," Mallarmé wrote, "there is the dream. It is the perfect use of this mystery which constitutes the symbol; to evoke an image little by little in order to show a state of soul." How responsive to his almost mystical teaching Vuillard is here. The deliberate lack of precision in this picture constitutes its principal charm. What the artist sees is filtered through thought and emotion, not to speak of his romantic attachment to Misia. The three figures can be identified. At the left, Misia, head bowed, appears to be bending over a piece of embroidery; in the center the playwright Romain Coolus extends himself sleepily in a Thonet chair, while, at the right, Thadée Natanson seems to doze over his reading, perhaps page proofs of the *Revue Blanche*. This magical scene sums up a whole chapter, both aesthetic and personal, in Vuillard's ardent youth.

Painted about 1898–1900

SYMPHONY IN RED

Oil on cardboard, 23 × 25 ³/₄"
Collection Mr. and Mrs. Ralph F. Colin, New York City

The suggested note here of the "naughtiness" of the 1890s is rarely found elsewhere in Vuillard's work of this early period, and never in later life. One would like to know more about this attractive dusky lady who sits stiffly yet seductively, wrapped in a loose scarlet dressing gown edged with marabou. There is something saucy, too, in the warm redness of the walls, not a favorite color, one may suspect, for the decoration of rooms in bourgeois circles. The whole sad gaiety of the characterization has great fascination. Stylistically, the painting is typically Nabi in its flatness, in the total ambiguity of space, and in the stagnant airlessness of the interior. But we remain perplexed by the lady who so easily dominates her exotic surroundings. Could she possibly be the actress Marthe Mellot, married to Alfred Natanson? She strongly resembles that lady (see their double portrait in the next color-plate), and the identification fits like a glove. For the nineties were the years of the *Revue Blanche* and Vuillard's intimacy with the whole Natanson family. Furthermore, during that decade he painted portraits only of his friends. Commissioned work for strangers lay well in the future. The date of execution of *Symphony in Red* is also somewhat perplexing. The manner is clearly that of Vuillard earlier in the decade, and the signed but undated picture has also been dated 1893. Further research may answer the question, but will not add to the intrinsic charm and value of this exceptional painting.

Painted 1900

ALFRED NATANSON
AND HIS WIFE

Oil on paper, 21 ¹/₄ × 26 ¹/₂"

Collection Nate B. and Frances Spingold, New York City

This spirited portrait belongs to the period when Vuillard's friendship with the whole Natanson family was at its closest. Alfred, one of the Natanson brothers, sons of a rich banker, had married the actress Marthe Mellot. The couple is portrayed in a casual, lively conversational duet more suggestive of a snapshot than of a lengthily pondered study. Vuillard derived this "modern" approach to sitters from the example of Degas, whom he greatly admired, and added his own intimist way of looking acutely at sitters. Nothing could be simpler, or stronger, than the dark patterning of contours and furniture against the whitewashed wall, an unusually severe scheme for Vuillard, who normally reveled in a profusion of soft, subtle colors. Turning, while making a remark to his amused wife, Alfred shows no more than an animated profile, vanishing as the head turns—that age-old convention in portraiture known as the *"profil perdu."* The double portrait is a discreet and charming souvenir of affectionate intimacy between the two of them and also reflects Vuillard's close involvement with these prized friends, and theirs with him.

Painted about 1900

THE CHAISE LONGUE

Distemper on cardboard, 23 ³/₄ × 24 ⁷/₈"
Collection Mr. and Mrs. Richard Rodgers, New York City

Few of Vuillard's paintings show more conspicuously than *The Chaise Longue* his altogether exceptional ability to incorporate so many disparate elements into a single unified design. Here he deliberately sets himself a problem that might have brought to grief a less crafty organizer of shape, color, and texture. One feels that these elements are definitely bound together by some internal relationship of whose mystery the relaxed lady reading the newspaper holds the key. She is not identified but evidently belonged to a richer and more sophisticated world than most of his other early sitters. Hence the artist's comparative detachment from her. She is obviously a woman of taste. We notice that she has thrown out of her drawing room all the Victorian furniture that must until recently have filled it, replacing it with handsome Louis XVI pieces, which the cultivated Paris world around 1900 was bringing back into fashion.

Painted 1900

WAITING (LA VISITE)

Oil on cardboard, 23 ¹/₂ × 20"
Collection E. G. Bührle, Zurich

In his characteristically overmodest way Vuillard frequently said that he was no more than an observer. True, he most often in his art withdraws from making comments or from any overt storytelling. Yet, occasionally, as in this solidly realized figure study, he achieves something more subtle and intangible than the "slice-of-life." For in his own manner he dramatizes this sitter. One cannot help wondering just what the solemn young woman has on her mind to lend her such a puzzled, troubled air. One feels that Vuillard's knowledge of the sitter is personal and deep, that he is trying to help her communicate some message, some explanation for her anxiety. This may well be a fanciful interpretation, but the artist does add a more eloquent dimension than we are accustomed to finding in matter-of-fact portraits. Furthermore, the title reminds us that the word *waiting* is one of the most poignant in the language. Quite a different point to be noticed here —and throughout Vuillard's work—is his expert eye for women's clothes. Not for nothing did he spend his youth in-and-out of his mother's shop. He notices every detail, catching the exact cut and texture of a dress, the way it fits, and catching, too, the fashionable tilt of a hat perched on an elaborate coiffure of the 1900s.

INTERIOR: WOMAN
BEFORE A WINDOW

Oil on panel, 24 $^3/_4$ × 22 $^3/_4$″
Private collection, New York City

Among the new friends made by Vuillard around the turn of the century was Madame Arthur Fontaine, the subject of this radiant portrait in which every touch of luscious, sun-drenched color is fresh and flickering. It signifies two novel elements in Vuillard's development. For the artist it represents a growing allegiance to the Impressionist mode of observation, where form is enlivened by being bathed in light and atmosphere and windows look out to the sky. It also marks his entry into the world of the rich, cultivated French upper bourgeoisie of which Madame Fontaine, wife of an important industrialist and sister-in-law of the composer Ernest Chausson, was a conspicuous member. In her Paris apartment near the Invalides she held musical gatherings attended by Claude Debussy, André Gide, Paul Valéry, Francis Jammes, Paul Claudel, and others. What we have here, as so often with Vuillard, is not so much a personal portrait—for the lady stands at farthest distance from the artist and turns away from him—as it is the portrait of a refined ambience, opulent yet distinguished. But how memorable she is, markedly slim, dressed in pink, light and almost transparent, her robe so artfully composed as to give an impression of warm splendor.

Painted about 1900

MOTHER AND CHILD

Oil on cardboard, 20 $^1/_8$ × 19 $^1/_4$"
Collection Mr. and Mrs. William Goetz, Los Angeles

By 1900 Vuillard had begun to simplify his interiors and, although this self-contained painting almost certainly represents his sister Madame Roussel and her daughter Annette, to reduce their emotional temperature. It will also be noticed how he has opened up pictorial space, frankly aiming at three-dimensional rendering that is only barely suggested in earlier work. This picture also makes us aware of the strength of the linear organization that underlies even his most elaborate portraits. The comparative simplicity here reveals the skeleton of design very well, and how skillfully he related shape to shape and color to color in the framework of design. The eye is drawn along the zig-zagging recession of the wall until it joins the red-brick interior of the fireplace confronting the young woman, also in red and determined not to give ground. A meeting of two immovable objects. Hence the noble, almost monumental simplicity and vitality of what might otherwise have been a conventional variation on the mother and child theme.

Painted 1903

ENTRANCE TO THE GARDEN

Oil on canvas, 23 × 30 ¹/₂"
Ittleson Collection, New York City

If, as a young Nabi, Vuillard rebelled against the Impressionists, agreeing with his revolutionary friends in their denunciation of Impressionist incoherence, uncritical observation of nature, refusal to use their minds—in short, their basically unintellectual approach to art—he was enthusiastically to renew their kind of lyrical vision in his work done between 1900 and 1914. In a lovely painting such as this, visual experiences are softly enveloped in the radiance of sunlight, color becomes iridescent, and sensation, rendered directly, owes almost everything to the early Monet. But not, it must be pointed out, to the relentless scientific Impressionism of Monet's haystacks or Rouen cathedrals, with which Vuillard was never in sympathy. However, he fully shared the older man's delight in the casual beauty of a modern domestic scene of the kind so lovingly depicted here. It is, of course, an intimist painting as well, a style Vuillard rarely relinquished. But now it becomes a muffled intimism, less sharp in its accents and less ambiguous in meaning, now increasingly involved in the sheer visual pleasures of the rich, comfortable world into which Lucie Hessel launched him.

Painted 1903

SELF-PORTRAIT

Oil on cardboard, $16\,^1/_8 \times 13\,^1/_8''$
Collection Mr. and Mrs. Donald S. Stralem, New York City

In this profoundly realized self-portrait, painted at the height of Vuillard's powers, we are confronted with nothing less than the peculiar innocence of the quintessentially private person. Its beauty is simply that of truth, arrived at in a search for self-knowledge and painted for himself alone. Vuillard was not primarily a face painter. Unlike Rembrandt, he did not focus on the face as the central psychological aspect of a sitter. He found other ways of achieving a likeness, building up an impression of character indirectly, and often giving less attention to the face than to other, apparently less important environmental details. But in his self-portraits nothing is allowed to divert our gaze from the artist's face, massive and dominating as nowhere else in his work. Unlike many self-portraits by other artists, who strike attitudes, let vanity, self-deceit, suppressed fantasies, and other aspects of temperament interfere with observation, Vuillard paints himself honestly. We feel that this is really what he looked like, not how he wanted to look. However, this portrait does not tell us much about the man behind the appearances. That Vuillard was reserved we know from the testimony of friends. That he was reserved even when communicating with himself through his work is demonstrated here.

Painted about 1904

CHILD LYING ON A RUG

Oil on panel, 14 ⁵/₈ × 20 ³/₄″

Collection Mrs. John Wintersteen, Villanova, Pennsylvania

Good painters often come to grief when painting children, when they cross, either deliberately or inadvertently, the razor's edge separating sentiment from sentimentality. But Vuillard knew children well and in this delightful picture he holds firmly to the side of reasonable sentiment. He even injects a good deal of tactful humor into this scene, where a golden-haired baby crawls helplessly across the rich Oriental rug, the only bit of human animation in the magnificent solemnity of the room with its superb formally arranged eighteenth-century French furniture. Obviously this little loved one is no member of the painter's family. It is possibly the child of one of Madame Hessel's friends, who must be anxiously watching the scene with a starched nurserymaid in attendance. The humor lies not only in the baby's bewilderment but in the subtlety with which Vuillard looks at the room through the eyes of a child, painting the furniture larger than life and seeing it mainly as a forest of legs. The compositional arrangement is exquisite, the sumptuous delicacy of color wholly remarkable, and the child far too natural and lively to risk becoming a doll woven into the pattern.

Painted about 1904

THE PAINTER KER-XAVIER
ROUSSEL AND HIS DAUGHTER

Oil on cardboard, 23 × 21″

Albright-Knox Art Gallery, Buffalo. Room of Contemporary Art Fund

Vuillard's earliest portraits depict his family and his intimates. And who ever was closer to him than K.-X. Roussel, doubly associated with Vuillard as his lifelong friend and brother-in-law. Indeed, Roussel's urging was largely responsible for Vuillard becoming a painter in the first place. He played a prominent role among the Nabis, collaborated with Vuillard at the Théâtre de l'Oeuvre, married Marie Vuillard, and was constantly thereafter a key figure in the close-knit family. Inseparable though they were, their painting paths went separate ways after 1900. Less gifted as an artist than Vuillard, Roussel, with more fantasy and less of a taste for realism, developed a high-spirited, neo-Baroque decorative style which he devoted to classical and mythological subject matter. He is little known outside of France, and even there not yet properly appreciated for the poetic artist that he was. Despite their close ties, Vuillard paints Roussel and his daughter Annette in a remarkably formal and impersonal way. It is one of the portraits that most strongly indicates Dutch influences on his work. Light bathes every object it encounters with beautiful impartiality and wraps the figures in silence.

Painted 1905

AT THE SEASHORE

Oil on panel, 8 ¹/₂ × 8 ¹/₂″

Collection Armand Hammer, Los Angeles

Three women held dominating positions in Vuillard's life. First and foremost his mother—he called her his "muse"—with whom he lived until her death in 1928. Then, for a few brief years late in the 1890s, the bewitching, capricious Misia Natanson breached the defences of his heart. Last, from 1900 on, he enjoyed an almost lover-like intimacy with Madame Jos Hessel, his dealer's wife, who in her quasi-maternal way virtually ran his life. This great friendship even aroused a slight jealousy on the part of the ever-devoted Madame Vuillard. Lucie Hessel, portrayed here at Amfreville in Normandy, had a robust, ardent, affectionate nature, and with her splendid efficiency and optimism energized his whole existence. She protected him and promoted his work, took him on trips abroad, had him to stay in the summer, entertained him almost every evening in Paris, and, after his mother's death, made a home for him at Les Clayes, her country house near Versailles. Some observers thought he occasionally chafed under her dominating ways, but on the whole he submitted to them willingly enough. Vuillard painted innumerable portraits of Madame Hessel, among which this rosy, summery evocation is perhaps the most charming. It convincingly demonstrates her personal fascination.

LE DIVAN ROUGE

Oil on canvas, 30 ¹/₄ × 27 ¹/₄" (sight)

Collection Mr. and Mrs. Albert K. Chapman, Rochester, New York

This luminous, freely handled, atmospheric picture of a lady posing on a sofa with casual grace portrays Madame Hessel in her apartment in the Rue de Rivoli. It would be wrong to consider this evocation of the familiar a portrait in the formal sense. Swimming light and color take complete control of the scene and the sitter. Vuillard never tired of painting Madame Hessel and her luxurious surroundings. One feels that here he willingly submits to a well-known, cherished subject without attempting to be too precise about the multiplicity of its elements. More than most of Vuillard's many other portraits of Lucie Hessel, this is an impression in the exact meaning of that word. Still, it would be interesting to be able to identify the pictures on the wall, for Jos Hessel was as avid a collector as he was a shrewd dealer, and he valued Vuillard's counsel when it came to buying for himself.

Painted 1908

THE ART DEALERS

Oil on canvas, 28 7/8 × 26"
City Art Museum of St. Louis

From 1899 to 1914 Vuillard exhibited at the Bernheim-Jeune Gallery in Paris, owned by the brothers Josse and Gaston Bernheim-Jeune, portrayed here at work in the gallery. They became his friends and found rich, discerning patrons for his work. Nonetheless, in portraits of them Vuillard apparently could not resist being something of a tease. He disdained the whole financial side of the art world; he was made uneasy by the high prices fetched by his work at the end of his life and, in portraits such as this, poked fun at high-powered dealers and their wiles. This witty double portrait verges on being a caricature of salesmanship techniques. While Josse does accounts in the background, Gaston stands ready to pounce on the next client, to dazzle him with sales talk and to blind him with that theatrical row of picture-lights.

Painted about 1908

INTERIOR OF A BEDROOM

Oil on cardboard, 23 × 24"

Collection Mr. and Mrs. Don Harrington, Amarillo, Texas

During the years around 1910 the Hessels would rent one summer house or another, usually near the sea in Brittany or Normandy, where rich Parisians could temporarily relax from their feverish urban existences. Almost invariably Vuillard followed them, either staying in the house or setting up a studio nearby. Just how halcyon such sojourns were is beautifully summed up in this sunny interior where Madame Hessel, busy at some household task, sits in her comfortable old-fashioned bedroom, whose big windows are thrown open to the green heat of summer. This everyday scene constitutes a hymn to the simple joy of living, accepting visual facts as they are and lending them an extra glow because of Madame Hessel's enlivening presence. Aside from her, the principal subject of this Impressionist picture, so lyrical in its sensuality, is reflected light and the way it illuminates a banal interior. Vuillard here generously repays his debt to Monet and paints what is for the time an old-fashioned picture, impossible to reconcile with the harsher and newer disciplines of Cubism and Fauvism then being practiced in avant-garde Paris circles.

Painted 1908–17

LA PLACE VINTIMILLE

Distemper on canvas, 63 $^1/_2$ × 90"

Collection Lita A. Hazen, New York City

Although Vuillard's name has become almost synonymous with the Place Vintimille (now Place Ad. Max), just off the Boulevard de Clichy, he and his mother did not live in that quarter until 1907, when they took an apartment at 26 Rue de Calais at the corner of the Place. Only in 1926 did they actually move into the tiny square itself—to 6 Place Vintimille. He obviously delighted in the view from his windows overlooking the leafy enclosure dominated by the statue of Hector Berlioz, who had lived nearby, and across to the shabby dignity of the yellowish houses also confronting the little public garden with its strollers and people sunning themselves. The artist continues his exploration of outdoor intimacy on a grand scale; but this is blander than earlier treatments of similar subject matter. It portrays a corner of the city he knew best, obviously preferable in his eyes to a banal and famous monument like the Arc de Triomphe. To Vuillard the sunny, dusty scene represented his personal microcosm of Paris, an oasis of calm in the heart of Montmartre, despite the fact that while he was painting it men working on some abyss in the street were in the process of tearing it up. But he painted ahead, through quiet and uproar, dominating all, communing knowingly with its friendliness and its peace, its existence an extension of himself. This wide view is an act of engaged observation made by a truly good and affectionate man.

Painted about 1910–12

MADAME HESSEL SEATED

Oil on canvas, 35 ³/₈ × 27 ¹/₂"
Collection Mrs. Lester Avnet, New York City

The idea of an abstract painting by Vuillard would rightly come as a total surprise to everyone. Yet, because of his lack of interest in dramatic incident, his passionate concern with relating on the picture surface each color, form, and trivial shape encountered by the eye, and his determination to absorb such details, large and small, into a coherent, lucid design, he sometimes comes close to abstraction. Nowhere, perhaps, more than in this picture (one can hardly call it a portrait) of his cherished friend Lucie Hessel seated in her Paris apartment at 33 Rue de Naples. Her pensive head counts for no more than any other observed incident in the chosen field of vision, no more, no less important than the pink-shaded lamp, the ceiling light reflected in the mirror, the mirror itself, the dim luster of the gold-framed paintings, and the pale tones of the brocaded furniture. Somehow, observing everything, subjecting everything to the demands of overall design, he brings it off. The results may be subtly rearranged but they remain true to facts. Art conceals artifice.

Painted 1912

THÉODORE DURET
IN HIS STUDY

Oil on cardboard, 37 1/2 × 29 1/2"
National Gallery of Art, Washington, D.C. Chester Dale Collection

Elderly sitters always appealed to Vuillard, who regarded age with particular tenderness and excelled in rendering its dignity and vulnerability. This majestic portrait of Théodore Duret (1838–1927) is one of his finest characterizations of those no longer young. It also pays tribute to a remarkable art critic, one of the first champions of Impressionism, whose book *Peintres Impressionistes* defended them unreservedly at a moment when they needed defenders. Manet was Duret's friend and particular hero. After the painter's death he was instrumental in the French government's acquisition of *Olympia,* and in 1912 he published the first definitive catalogue of Manet's work. In this portrayal, the now feeble old gentleman, grave as a Venetian Doge, sits holding his cat Lulu, in poignant contrast with his youthful portrait by Whistler (1883), which can be seen reflected in the mirror in the upper right-hand corner. In painting Duret, surrounded by his books and some of the works he helped bring to fame, Vuillard paints not only a portrait of the man but a pictorial biography as well.

Painted 1918

ANNETTE MEDITATING

Distemper on canvas, 29 × 27 ¹/₂″
Private collection, Paris

No artist, even the conservative Vuillard, fails from time to time to surprise us. Just when we become accustomed to portraits where backgrounds and accessories play an almost larger part in the general effect than the sitter, Vuillard will suddenly paint a portrait, such as this of his niece Annette Roussel, where he concentrates sharply on the features and hardly bothers, except in the most casual manner, to brush in the figure and the background. We know that the young girl, so vividly and concretely characterized in the deep gaze she directs at the artist, is seated at a table in a room, but nothing else. He repays her look with an active curiosity, fixing her features with incisive draftsmanship as they come before his penetrating eye. This brilliantly observed study, deriving in style from Degas, portrays a familiar, beloved member of his family and makes a rare psychological comment on the subject of adolescence as well. It is obvious that Annette's personality and development were of special importance to her uncle, who almost never ventured into the kind of searching intimacy that is so palpable here.

Painted 1926

MADAME VUILLARD
AT THE WINDOW

Pastel, 25 5/8 × 18 7/8"

Private collection, Paris

By the time this infinitely touching portrait—one of the very last of so many in a series stretching back for forty years—was painted, Madame Vuillard was indeed very old, being well into her eighties, although that loving, protective, generous life did not come to an end until December 1928. It is a Dutch picture, this silent, sunny, warm interior where the old lady, busy as always with her hands, sits in the stillness, only now and then aware of the bustle of other generations in the Place Vintimille outside. She had fully earned the rewards of a happy old age, and of nothing in her contented existence was she prouder than the fame of the devoted son who had never left her side. "I shall never forget," wrote Thadée Natanson, who knew her well, "the tone of voice in which she would say, 'Am I not his mother?' " As a portrait it is naturally one of peculiarly intense intimacy. And, as was his custom, while focusing on the bowed figure Vuillard takes meticulous account of the familiar surroundings which round out the central act of portraiture. He even goes so far as to complete the picture by showing, in the big mirror, a reflection of a corner of the room we do not see. And color, a subtle profusion of autumnal hues, ideally matches the artist's reverential feelings toward the subject.

Painted about 1930

STUDY FOR THE PORTRAIT
OF BONNARD

Distemper on paper mounted on canvas, $44\,^7/_8 \times 57\,^1/_2''$
Musée du Petit-Palais, Paris

Closely linked during their lifetimes, the names of Bonnard and Vuillard come down together in history. Next to Roussel, Bonnard was Vuillard's most intimate friend—fellow-student at the Académie Julian, co-sharer of a studio in 1890, and equally prominent among the Nabis and in the circle of the *Revue Blanche*. In the beginning he painted in a similar manner to Vuillard. Their styles soon differed, however, although both can be considered late Impressionists. Bonnard was the more aesthetically adventurous of the two, with a passion for landscape and often for a capricious subject matter not to be met in Vuillard's more conservative and urbane style of painting with its emphasis on portraiture, a field largely ignored by Bonnard. But nothing disturbed their long and well-established friendship. This vivid sketch, preparatory to a finished portrait (also in the Petit-Palais), has been well described by Claude Roger-Marx. "Standing in profile," he writes, "thin, in neat morning dress, Bonnard inspects a large landscape pinned to the wall. In another minute, one guesses, he will ransack the magic box— the box of colours before him on the table. Like a commander who searches the horizon, he stands, face to face with this picture, which is a mirror, prepared to take a step backward. Wonderingly, his basset hound seated on a low divan contemplates with comic absorption his silent, trans- ported, hallucinated master. The dialogue between the author and his work fills a world of enchantment. Yet this is only one of those undistinguished modern drawing rooms with bare walls in which Bonnard chose to paint. All the golds, all the blond tints, all the rich colours which go to the com- position of his works have transfigured, one might think, this room so paradoxically consecrated to the arts." Actually the scene takes place in Bonnard's studio at Le Cannet, and the unidentified landscape depicts the hinterlands of High Provence.

Painted 1931

THE VISIT

Mixed technique on canvas, 39 ³/₈ × 53 ³/₄″

The National Gallery of Art, Washington, D.C. Chester Dale Collection

Of the forty or more commissioned portraits Vuillard painted after 1920, usually at the inducement of the Hessels, this is one of the most accomplished and elaborately finished. It also belongs among those giving ammunition to his critics, one of whom summed up the current point of view by writing that Vuillard "took to naturalistic portraiture of women . . . not because he hankered after smart society, but out of some misguided self-effacement, with the result that sometimes the subject of his picture slipped from his grasp and took charge. With nothing to fall back on but good taste and honest vision, which embraced too many commonplace objects, the personality of the painter fades, and we are left with nothing but a timid reconstruction, very valuable no doubt to the social historian." There is truth in this charge. After the flight of youth, and confronted with sitters he neither knew well nor cared much about, he could and did lapse into a dull academic manner. In defense of Vuillard's no more than talented professionalism of later years one can point out that he remained much too fine an artist ever to be dismissed out of hand. Again and again one can discern in these late portraits, their loss of sparkle and of real involvement with the sitter notwithstanding, what a learned painter he continued to be until the end. Nor can they be ignored in any serious consideration of his career. One cannot but admire, for example, how the lamplight in this triple intimist portrait unites not only the sitters but the whole opulent décor as well. And as for its value as a social document relating to upper middle-class French life between the two World Wars, there can be little question. Actually it is surprising that this portrait should not be more intimate and informal than it is, for it portrays, on the right, none other than Madame Hessel, now white-haired, to whom her friend, Madame Léopold Marchand, on the left, is paying the visit. And the setting, certainly familiar enough to Vuillard, is the Hessels' Paris apartment, 33 Rue de Naples.

LA COMTESSE DE NOAILLES

Oil on canvas, 43 ¹/₂ × 50 ¹/₂"

Collection Hon. and Mrs. Samuel J. LeFrak, New York City

This portrait, existing in several versions, gave Vuillard more trouble than almost any other. Time and again he would return to Madame de Noailles's apartment, 40 Rue Scheffer, to verify this detail or that, making innumerable sketches of the hands, the flowered coverlet, even of the speaking tube, all of which studies furnished raw material for the finished portrait that, as was his custom, he created wholly in the studio. When completed, some acclaimed it a masterpiece while others placed it on a far lower level, complaining about the vulgar, flashy color and about Vuillard's increasing interest in trivial detail. Anna de Noailles herself noticed the artist's encyclopedic observation. "For heaven's sake hide that tube of vaseline," she would cry. "M. Vuillard paints everything he sees."

Whether the final aesthetic verdict on the painting is favorable or not, one can only be grateful that Vuillard undertook the task of portraying this famous lady, an almost neurotically brilliant writer who flashed like a meteor across the skies of the social and literary worlds of Paris during the first quarter of the twentieth century. Of mixed Greek, Turkish, and Romanian blood, married into one of the very grandest French families, this exotic genius took the world by storm because of her beauty, her literary gifts, and her amazing, near-hypnotic powers of conversation. Maurice Barrès, reported to have been her lover, described her as "the most sensitive point in the universe," and although the impassioned romanticism of her poetry may nowadays have gone out of fashion it will not necessarily remain so. Vuillard painted this portrait the year before her death at the age of fifty-seven. She was already ill, but had the habit of receiving people in her bedroom as she reclined in her big Louis XVI bed, alternately languorous and excessively vital. "I never knew a girl to toss about in bed so," said the novelist Abel Hermant. This whirlwind could not have been an easy sitter for Vuillard, but the results of their encounter will for long be of the greatest fascination.

SELECTED BIBLIOGRAPHY

GENERAL WORKS

Blanche, Jacques-Emile. *Les Arts Plastiques sous la Troisième République.* Paris: Les Editions de France, 1931.

Chassé, Charles. *The Nabis and Their Period.* Translated by Michael Bullock. New York–Washington: Frederick A. Praeger, 1969.

Denis, Maurice. *Théories 1890–1910: Du Symbolisme et de Gauguin vers un nouvel ordre classique.* Paris: Bibliothèque de l'Occident, 1912.

———. *Nouvelles Théories sur l'art moderne. Sur l'art sacré, 1914–1921.* Paris: Rouart et Watelin, 1922.

Dorival, Bernard. *Twentieth Century Painters: Nabis, Fauves, Cubists.* New York: Universe, 1958.

Geffroy, Gustave. *La Vie artistique.* Vol. II, Paris: E. Dentu, 1893. Vol. VI, Paris: H. Floury, 1900.

Humbert, Agnès. *Les Nabis et leur époque, 1888–1900.* Geneva: Pierre Cailler, 1954.

Huyghe, René, ed. *Histoire de l'art contemporain: La Peinture.* Paris: Alcan, 1935. *"Les Nabis"* by Bazin, Chassé, Dupont, Fegdal, Huyghe, Sterling.

Huyghe, René. *Les Contemporains.* Paris: Tisné, 1939.

Lugné-Poë, Aurélien. *La Parade. II. Acrobaties, souvenirs et impressions du théâtre, 1894–1902.* Paris: Nouvelle Revue Française, 1931.

Natanson, Thadée. *Peints à leur tour.* Paris: Albin Michel, 1948.

Nattier-Natanson, E. *Les Amitiés de la Revue Blanche et quelques autres.* Vincennes: Les Editions du Donjon, 1959.

Painter, George. *Marcel Proust.* 2 vols. Boston: Little, Brown, 1959–65.

Rewald, John. *Post-Impressionism from Van Gogh to Gauguin.* New York: The Museum of Modern Art, 1956, revised 1962.

Segard, Achille. *Peintres d'aujourd'hui. Les Décorateurs.* Paris: Ollendorf, 1914.

Sert, Misia. *Misia and the Muses.* New York: John Day, 1953.

Sérusier, Paul. *ABC de la Peinture, suivi d'une étude sur la vie et l'oeuvre de Paul Sérusier par Maurice Denis.* Paris: Floury, 1942. First edition 1921, second edition 1950, with correspondence collected by Madame Sérusier.

Verkade, Dom Willibrord (Jan). *Yesterdays of an Artist-Monk.* Translated from German by John L. Stoddard. London: Burns, Oates & Washbourne. New York: Kenedy, 1930.

Vollard, Ambroise. *Recollections of a Picture Dealer.* Boston: Little, Brown, 1936.

Werth, Léon. *Quelques Peintres.* Paris: G. Crès, 1921.

BIOGRAPHIES AND MONOGRAPHS

Chastel, André. *Vuillard: 1868–1940.* Paris: Floury, 1946.

———. *Vuillard, peintures, 1890–1930.* Paris: Les Editions du Chêne, 1948.

Giraudoux, Jean. *Le Tombeau d'Edouard Vuillard.* Paris: Daragnès, 1944. With 5 original etchings. *Pour les amis de Vuillard.*

Mercanton, Jacques. *Vuillard et le goût du bonheur.* Paris: A. Skira, 1949.

Roger-Marx, Claude. *Vuillard: His Life and Work.* Translated by E. B. D'Auvergne. New York: Editions de La Maison Française, 1946.

———. *Vuillard: Intérieurs.* Paris: La Bibliothèque des Arts, 1968.

Salomon, Jacques. *Vuillard, témoignage.* Paris: Albin Michel, 1945.

———. *Auprès de Vuillard.* Paris: La Palme, 1953.

———. *Vuillard admiré.* Paris: La Bibliothèque des Arts, 1961.

———. *Vuillard.* Paris: Gallimard, 1968.

ARTICLES

Denis, Maurice. "L'Epoque du Symbolisme." *Gazette des Beaux-Arts* (Paris), 854, March 1934.

Gide, André. "Promenade au Salon d'Automne." *Gazette des Beaux-Arts* (Paris), 582, December 1905.

Rewald, John. "Extraits du Journal inédit de Paul Signac." *Gazette des Beaux-Arts* (Paris), 36, July–September 1949; 39, April 1952.

EXHIBITION CATALOGUES
(chronologically arranged)

London: Wildenstein. *Edouard Vuillard.* June 1948. Text by Claude Roger-Marx.

New York: The Museum of Modern Art. *Edouard Vuillard.* April 6–June 6, 1954, in collaboration with The Cleveland Museum of Art, January 26–March 14, 1954. Essay "Edouard Vuillard" by Andrew Carnduff Ritchie, "Notes on Vuillard as a Printmaker" by William S. Lieberman, Bibliography by Bernard Karpel.

London: Marlborough Gallery. *Roussel: Bonnard: Vuillard.* May 5–June 12, 1954. Preface by John Russell, texts by G. Geffroy, P. Signac, M. Denis, A. Gide.

New Haven: Yale University Art Gallery. *Neo-Impressionists and Nabis in the Collection of Arthur G. Altschul.* January 20–March 14, 1965. Robert L. Herbert, Editor; William E. Mitchell, Associate Editor.

Paris: Orangerie des Tuileries. *Edouard Vuillard: K.-X. Roussel.* May 28–September 16, 1968, in collaboration with Haus der Kunst, Munich, March 16–May 12, 1968. Essay "Propos sur l'amitié de K.-X. Roussel et Edouard Vuillard" by Jacques Salomon, Preface by Claude Roger-Marx, Biography by Antoine Salomon, Catalogue by Pierre Georgel.